Physical Characteristics
of the Bearded Collie

(from the American Kennel Club breed standard)

Back: Level.

Tail: Set low and is long enough for the end of the bone to reach at least the point of the hocks. The tail is covered with abundant hair.

Hindquarters: The hind legs are powerful and muscular at the thighs with well bent stifles. The hocks are low. The legs are covered with shaggy hair all around.

Coat: Double with the undercoat soft, furry and close. The outercoat is flat, harsh, strong and shaggy.

Size:
The ideal height at the withers is 21–22 inches for adult dogs and 20–21 inches for adult bitches.

Color: All Bearded Collies are born either black, blue, brown or fawn, with or without white markings.

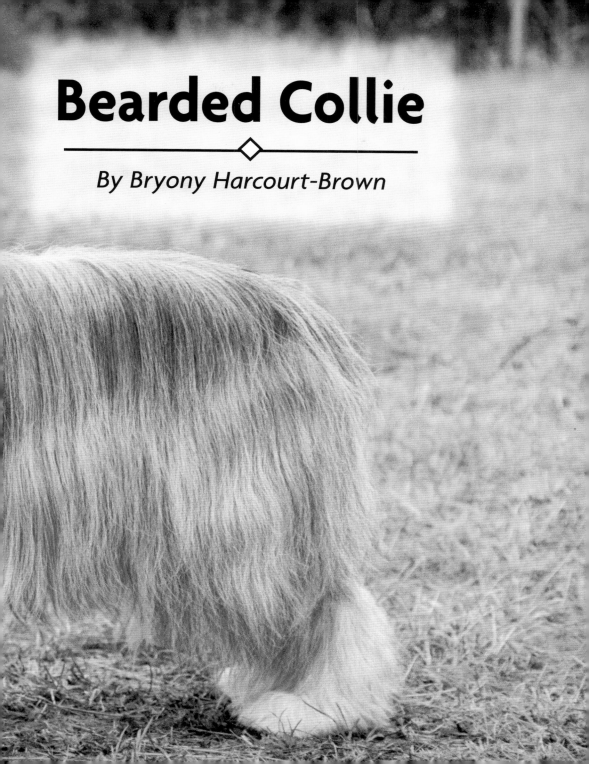

Bearded Collie

◇

By Bryony Harcourt-Brown

Contents

Training Your Bearded Collie   **86**

Begin with the basics of training the puppy and adult dog. Learn the principles of house-training the Bearded Collie, including the use of crates and basic scent instincts. Get started by introducing the pup to his collar and leash and progress to the basic commands. Find out about obedience classes and other activities.

Healthcare of Your Bearded Collie   **110**

By Lowell Ackerman DVM, DACVD
Become your dog's healthcare advocate and a well-educated canine keeper. Select a skilled and able veterinarian. Discuss pet insurance, vaccinations and infectious diseases, the neuter/spay decision and a sensible, effective plan for parasite control, including fleas, ticks and worms.

Showing Your Bearded Collie   **138**

Step into the center ring and find out about the world of competitive events for pure-bred dogs. Here's an overview of AKC conformation and some popular performance events for Bearded Collies: obedience trials, agility, herding events and tracking.

Behavior of Your Bearded Collie   **144**

Analyze the canine mind to understand what makes your Bearded Collie tick. How to handle common problems, including jumping up, barking, different types of aggression, separation anxiety, sex-related behaviors, digging and more, is discussed.

KENNEL CLUB BOOKS: BEARDED COLLIE
ISBN: 1-59378-236-5

Copyright © 2005 • Kennel Club Books, LLC
308 Main Street, Allenhurst, NJ 07711 USA
Cover Design Patented: US 6,435,559 B2 • Printed in South Korea

Photography by:

Paulette Braun, T.J. Calhoun, Alan and Sandy Carey, Carolina Biological Supply, Isabelle Français, Bryony Harcourt-Brown, Carol Ann Johnson, Bill Jonas, Dr. Dennis Kunkel, Tam C. Nguyen, Phototake, Jean Claude Revy, Steven Surfman, Karen Taylor, Michael Martin Trafford, Alice van Kempen and Meryel Wood.

Illustrations by Renée Low and Patricia Peters.

The publisher wishes to thank all of the owners of the dogs featured in this book.

Many people feel attracted to the Bearded Collie because of its "shaggy-dog" appeal. The Beardie is a handsome pure-bred through and through with a long history as a working sheep and cattle dog.

BEARDED COLLIE

The Bearded Collie is very much the type of breed that many people feel they already know, simply because of its similarity to a lot of "shaggy dog" types. Until comparatively recently, however, many people did not know the name of the breed when they met one and would often confuse the Bearded Collie with the Old English Sheepdog. Despite the similar shaggy appearance and herding heritage, the breeds are actually very different in body

The basic shape and balance of early Bearded Collies should be evident in quality examples of the breed today. This is the author's Eng. Ch. Chriscaro Chrystal at Orora at three years of age.

THE BEARDIE APPEARS

Shaggy dogs of similar type to the Beardie first began appearing in art and books in the early 19th century. Two different paintings entitled "The Shepherd's Dog," one by P. Reinagle in about 1803 and the other by W. Barraud dated 1854, show dogs of definite Beardie type. It is possible these Scottish dogs evolved from other shaggy flock-gathering breeds on the Continent such as the Pyrenean Sheepdog, the Portuguese Sheepdog, the Catalan Sheepdog and, the most likely ancestor, the Polish Lowland Sheepdog. Legends state that some of these dogs arrived in the United Kingdom on ships and were traded like other stock and produce.

and head shape, general construction and overall balance.

The Bearded Collie has, in fact, a long history in various guises but all rather similar to the dogs we still see nowadays. Grooming techniques may result in longer and, often, heavier coats, but the basic shape and balance of the early Beardies are, or should be, still there.

In the beginning, there were no Bearded Collies, and it was a dull world indeed. Eventually, people who owned sheep noticed that the sheep were troublesome to keep in one place, and few people could run fast enough to gather them. And so the herding dog was born! At first, shepherds used dogs of any type that would gather. Then they began to notice that certain types of these dogs were also good playmates for their children. Some were hardy and worked better than other types in their given environments and climates. And some were just plain fun to have around, as well as good workers…and so the Beardie came into being. And the world became more fun!

The Bearded Collie originated in Britain as a working sheep and cattle dog. It is generally accepted that the Bearded Collie's temperament was ideally suited to the work of a drover, often covering great distances to drive cattle safely to market over rough terrain. This would certainly be borne out by the Bearded Collie's method of working stock, which typically displays a rough-and-ready attitude, nudging and nipping the heels and coaxing the livestock into order. This behav-

Author Bryony Harcourt-Brown with her first Bearded Collie, a lovely chocolate and white, who converted the author to the Beardie fold.

ior is still readily evident in present-day Beardies, given the opportunity.

Some years ago, one of my Beardie bitches displayed her instinct with cattle in a most daredevil and courageous act, herding and removing some beasts that had broken out of their field and were making attempts to chase me on my pony. Despite my cries to her to come away, she took them to the far end of the field and rejoined me only when she could see that we were out of any danger. This was a show bitch, long removed from working stock, who had never been tried with any form of work. Beardies running with other dogs or, indeed, with their family members will also often display herding instinct, maintaining a

BARKING BEARDIES
In many parts of Britain, working Beardies were known as "Barking Dogs" due to their habit of continually barking as they worked. You may wish to consider this if you are thinking of acquiring your first Beardie. It is a trait that they have not lost over the generations!

Early Beardie types were known by a variety of names such as the Scotch Sheepdog and the Hairy Mou'ed Collie. In the South of England, there were also dogs famed as drovers, of Beardie type, known as Smithfields. These were so named as they were used by drovers to take cattle to London's Smithfield Market. The Smithfields were famous for their ability to find their own way home, passing from farm to farm along the way. Interestingly, there are still working dogs bearing the name Smithfield in Tasmania today.

Other mention has been made of dogs known as the "Barking Dogs" or "Noisy Dogs," which seem to have been of Beardie type and possibly had been used by the Celtic people in early British history. Wherever mention of this type of dog is made, various qualities have also repeatedly been attributed to them. These include their capacity for independent thought and their intelligence,

constant eye on their "charges" and constantly circling and checking the course of their playmates.

Various theories have been propounded as to the original breeds that formed the Beardie, but none of these theories has been satisfactorily proved due to a lack of written documentation. Nevertheless, it is generally accepted that dogs of hairy type with exceptional abilities with sheep and cattle and of a hardy disposition were highly prized in Scotland. These dogs may have derived from a number of sources, including some of the Eastern European breeds. However, it is most likely that the Bearded Collie predominantly gained ancestry from a number of native breeds and not from any one breed in particular.

COLLIE COUSIN
One of the "breeds" considered by many to be an early Beardie cousin was called the Smithfield. Dogs called Smithfields, with a number of characteristics similar to those of Bearded Collies, are a highly prized working breed still being used for sheep and cattle by farmers in Tasmania. These dogs, like Beardies, give voice while working.

The Collie (on the right), is the more familiar "collie," though the Bearded Collie is growing in popularity by leaps and bounds.

allowing them to work without direction and bring home lost sheep without assistance. Another constant is the description of the dogs using "plenty of voice," an attribute that allowed the whereabouts of the dogs to remain known despite their being out of sight. These qualities meant that

HIGH ACHIEVERS

The first Bearded Collie to achieve the prestigious title of Obedience Champion in Britain was Obedience Champion Scapa, by Eng. Ch. Bosky Glen of Bothkennar out of Swalehall Martha Scrope. Scapa was owned and trained by Jenni (Cooke) Wiggins.

In the early 1970s, the Beardie gained its first obedience title in the US through Ch. Brambledale Blue Bonnet, CD, ROM, also the breed's first conformation champion. Ch. OTCh. Windcache A Briery Bess later was the first to achieve the lofty title of Obedience Trial Champion.

the Beardie type of worker was very highly prized.

Despite all historical references to dogs of Beardie type throughout Britain, the Bearded Collie is generally known as a Scottish breed, and certainly it was from Scotland that the history is taken up in more modern and well-documented times.

Although still in existence, the Bearded Collie became largely forgotten as the years passed. The need for a long-distance drover had become all but obsolete with more modern methods of sending sheep and cattle to market.

In 1944, Mrs. G. O. Willison, a lady from England, wished to procure a Shetland Sheepdog from working stock and negotiated the purchase of such an animal from Scotland. In fact, she was sent a chocolate (brown) bitch puppy, which later proved to be a Bearded Collie.

Having researched the matter, Mrs. Willison set about trying to breed from this bitch, Jeannie. The first litter, to a half-bred Beardie male, was not a success and none of the resultant puppies were retained. However, Mrs. Willison was able to register Jeannie by a no-longer-used method that, at the time, allowed a judge to certify breed type and quality in a specific animal in order for it to gain English Kennel Club registration. Jeannie was registered as Jeannie of Bothkennar.

Despairing of ever finding a suitable Beardie mate for Jeannie, Mrs. Willison happened by sheer chance to meet a slate-and-white Bearded Collie dog and his owner on Hove Beach, Sussex, England. As the dog required a new home at that time, Mrs. Willison acquired him, and he was registered as Bailie of Bothkennar. Jeannie and Bailie produced their litter in 1950 and Mrs. Willison kept four pups: three males, one named Bogle of Bothkennar; and a female.

A year later, Mrs. Willison obtained Bess of Bothkennar from Argyll in Scotland. Bess was mated to Bogle and produced a bitch, Briery Nan of Bothkennar, who was to feature frequently in later pedigrees. Another outcross was Newtown Blackie; this dog, when mated to Briery Nan, produced Ridgeway Rob, a famous early male. Although there were other dogs brought in, the extent of the early available breeding stock was extremely limited. Consequently, it is probable that all modern-day Kennel-Club-registered Bearded Collies are descended from Jeannie and Bailie's original combination.

Miss K. Suzanne Moorhouse, of the renowned Willowmead kennels, obtained Eng. Ch. Willowmead Barberry of Bothkennar from Mrs. Willison. Barberry's litter brother, Eng. Ch. Wishanger Barley of Bothkennar, was owned by Miss Mary Partridge, famous for the Wishanger Beardies. Miss Partridge also obtained a bitch from Miss Moorhouse, Eng. Ch. Willowmead My Honey, who, when mated to Eng. Ch. Barley, produced Eng. Ch. Wishanger Cairnbhan, another highly influential early stud dog.

In 1959, the first Challenge Certificates (awards that count toward a British championship) for the breed were awarded at Britain's famed Crufts show, and the Best of Breed winner was Beauty Queen of Bothkennar, who quickly became the first champion Bearded Collie.

A few years later, another up-and-coming breeder obtained Bothkennar stock. Miss Shirley Holmes, who was to become well known and respected for her Edenborough Beardies, obtained Eng. Ch. Bracken Boy of Bothkennar, born in 1962 and who was to produce some influential offspring.

Owing to ill health, Mrs. Willison began to reduce her involvement in the breed, parting with many of her dogs, and in 1964 the highly successful Bothkennar kennel was finally disbanded.

REVIVING THE BREED
But for the tireless work of Mrs. G. O. Willison, the Bearded Collie as we know it might not be around today. Mrs. Willison is generally credited with the revival of the breed.

This is Eng. Ch. Mignonette of Willowmead at Orora, who was the Top Bearded Collie in Britain in 1975 and 1976.

isles, Tambora, Broadholme, Beagold and Chantala.

My own first Bearded Collies, obtained in the beginning of the 1970s, were from the Osmart and Willowmead kennels. My Osmart bitch actually still carried unknown breeding on one side of her pedigree. I also obtained a bitch of working origins, although Kennel-Club-registered, from Scotland. These three, with a bitch by Eng. Ch. Edenborough Blue Bracken, formed the foundation of my kennel. The bitch I bought from Miss Moorhouse became Eng. Ch. Mignonette of Willowmead at Orora, who was Top Bearded Collie in Britain for 1975 and 1976. Mignonette was by Eng. Ch. Wishanger Cairnbhan. When mated to Eng. Ch. Osmart Bonnie Blue Braid, Mignonette produced Eng. Ch. Orora's Frank, who is behind so many of today's dogs. Frank was Top Bearded Collie for 1983 and 1984.

Another dog carrying Wishanger lines was Mike and Janet Lewis's Eng. Ch. Pepperland Lyric John at Potterdale. "Lyric John," the first major Potterdale show dog, was to start a phenomenal show career for Janet and Mike. They have produced innumerable top-quality champions in the breed, including Brenda White's lovely Eng. Ch. Potterdale Classic of Moonhill, the 1989 Crufts Best-in-Show winner, who was sired by Eng. Ch. Orora's Frank.

Ken and Jenny Osborne had obtained Eng. Ch. Blue Bonnie of Bothkennar from Mrs. Willison in 1963, followed by Eng. Ch. Bravo of Bothkennar in 1964. Although Ken and Jenny already had Bluebelle of Bothkennar, Bravo and Blue Bonnie really became the foundation of the Osmart kennel, a very famous kennel with many champions to its name. Probably the most influential of these champions would be Eng. Ch. Osmart Bonnie Blue Braid, by Eng. Ch. Bravo out of Eng. Ch. Blue Bonnie. This wonderful blue male was to make a major impact on the breed, as was Miss Shirley Holmes's Eng. Ch. Edenborough Blue Bracken, grandson of the aforementioned Eng. Ch. Bracken Boy of Bothkennar and the top-winning Beardie for many years as well as the breed's first Best-in-Show winner.

Other famous kennels responsible for champions in 1960s Britain included Cannamoor, Brambledale, Davealex, Western-

BEARDIES IN THE US AND BEYOND

By Chris Walkowicz

Although Bearded Collies were probably exported from Britain in the early part of the 20th century, the main exportation of Beardies from Britain seems to have begun in the late 1950s. Popular in the United States, Canada, Australia, New Zealand, Europe and Asia, the breed continues to gain footholds wherever a Beardie charms his way into a home and heart.

Two Beardies out of a litter sired by Ridgeway Rob out of Bra'Tawney of Bothkennar were the first known of the breed to enter the United States, this in 1957. They landed in Connecticut and were undoubtedly good companions but were never shown, and no record exists of their being bred. In 1967, the first litter of Bearded Collies was registered with the American Kennel Club (AKC), bred by Larry and Maxine Levy of Heathglen kennels. The Levys had owned and shown the breed in Europe.

The Bearded Collie Club of America (BCCA) was founded in 1969 with five members. Larry Levy served as the first president of the organization. Members accepted the British breed standard as the official standard by which the breed would be judged.

The shaggy, fun-loving, winsome Bearded Collie quickly attracted new fanciers and, by the following year, the club boasted 45 members. That year, 12 litters were whelped, with 19 imports and 32 American-bred dogs that were registered by D. Ian Morrison, BCCA registrar. Two hundred Beardies were added to the registry books in the first three years of the club's existence, a sign of the breed's appeal.

Within a short time, D. Ian and Moira Morrison became Beardie breeders under the Cauldbrae name, with Tom and Barbara Davies's Dunwich Beardies following close after the Levys' and Morrisons'. Richard and Linda Nootbaar (Rich-Lin) and Anne Dolan (Glen Eire) soon had litters of Beardies as well. After these five pioneer families, several others became enamored of the

MOVERS AND SHAKERS

Among the top-producing kennels in the breed's early years in the US were Arcadia, Artisan, Gaymardon, Ha'Penny, Parcana and Silverleaf. During the second decade, Arlin, Brandmar, Briarpatch, Brigadoon, Britannia, Chelsic, Ragtyme, Southampton, Stonehaven and Windfiddler were among the kennels that produced many lovely Beardies. Most of these kennels are still active today. Once a Beardie lover, always a Beardie lover!

breed, and 1974 saw a flurry of Beardie litters and an emergence of breeders: Virginia Parsons (Braemoor), Freedo and Barbara Rieseberg (Silverleaf), Robert and Henrietta Lachman (Cricket) and J. Richard and Barbara Schneider (Ha'Penny). Tom Davies, Virginia Parsons, J. Richard Schneider and the Lachmans are still members of the BCCA.

Just seven short years after the founding of the BCCA, the Bearded Collie was accepted by the American Kennel Club for competition in the Miscellaneous Class. Shortly thereafter, the breed was admitted into the AKC Stud Book. Due to their allure, Beardies moved swiftly toward full recognition and trotted into the Working Group in 1977. A year later, an amended breed standard was authored by Tom Davies and Moira Morrison and approved by the BCCA and the AKC.

Ch. Brambledale Blue Bonnet, CD, ROM swiftly became the first AKC champion for our breed, as well as the first obedience-titled Beardie. Bonnet was imported in 1972 by J. Richard Schneider and

THE HISTORY OF BEARDIE FIRSTS

• *Ch. Brambledale Blue Bonnet CD, ROM:* First Beardie conformation champion and obedience titlist in the US, first Beardie Group and Best in Show (BIS) winner in the US and first Beardie Best of Breed (BOB) winner at the Westminster Kennel Club show (1978).

• *Am./Can./Int. Ch. Diotima Bear Necessity CD, HC, CGC, ROM, ROMI, VA:* First Group winner at Westminster. *Eng./Can. Ch. Edenborough Kara Kara of Josanda:* BOB winner at the BCCA's first national specialty (1979).

• *Ch. Rich-Lin's Molly of Arcadia, ROMX:* Top Bearded Collie dam and all-breeds.

• *Am./Can. Ch. Windfiddler's Still Cruisin HIC, ROMX, ROMAX, ROMIX, ROMOX, ROMH:* Top sire.

• *Ch. HC WTCh. Britannia Chip Thrills UDX, MX, MXJ, ASCA UD, HRDIIIs, MV, TDI, CGC, ROMX, ROMAX:* First Herding Champion and first Master in Versatility title. Only four dogs have attained their herding championships: Chip; *Am./Can. Ch. HC WTCh. Glen Elder Silver Artisan RTDsc, HRDIIIs; HC Artisan Starlight* and *Ch. HC Artisan Northern Night.*

• *Ch. OTCh. Windcache A Briery Bess:* First Obedience Trial Champion and one of the only two Beardie obedience champions, along with first *OTCh./UDX Ch. OTCh. Walkoway's Frosted Flakes UDX, OA, NAC, NJC, STDs, HS, HIT, CGC.*

• *Am./Can. Ch. Britannia Back To The Future AX, MXJ, RN:* First Rally title.

• *Ch. Oakengates Havin' a Ball TDX:* First TDX.

• *Ch. MACH Balgrae's Sean Mackay CD, HS, STDs, JHDs, NAC, NJC, VX:* First Master Agility Champion (MACH).

• *MACH4 O'Duinnin HMT Sonic Boom AAD, EAC, EJC, OGC:* Appropriately named, "Jet" has a quadruple MACH title.

was owned by him and the Lachmans for a few years, after which the Lachmans became sole owners.

In 1983, the Beardie joined the other herding breeds when the Herding Group was formed. The breed increased quickly in popularity. Beardie devotees are thankful, however, that it has not reached the top 10 or 20 breeds. It remains steadily around the halfway mark in the AKC's registration statistics of its 160-plus breeds.

The very things that attract the breed's fanciers—the Beardie's

Two British-born champions, Eng. Ch. Chriscaro Chrystal at Orora and Eng. Ch. Orora's Laughing Waters.

FOR THE LOVE OF THE BEARDIE...

Although the AKC Bearded Collie breed standard has not been changed since 1978, an illustrated standard was approved by the BCCA in 2002. The illustrations by Chet Jezierski and the expanded text by the BCCA Judges Education Committee have received rave reviews from judges and fanciers alike.

In addition to the national club, there are also regional Beardie clubs around the US. These can be found by contacting the AKC or checking the BCCA's website at http://beardie.net/bcca.

In addition, an independent organization, Bearded Collie Foundation for Health (BeaCon), has an open registry for Beardies with the purpose of gathering information for health research. The website for BeaCon is http://beaconforhealth.org.

effervescent personality, activity level, independent thinking and beautiful coat (requiring regular care)—are the same characteristics that are turn-offs for others. Unfortunately, not everyone considers these traits when falling for the fuzzy face of a baby Beardie, resulting in some Beardies' being given up by their owners, who were not prepared to meet the requirements of Bearded Collie ownership. Thus, in 1985, at Paul Glatzer's suggestion and direction, the BCCA began its successful rescue program. To date, hundreds of Beardies have been placed in new homes, thanks to Paul Glatzer and his dozens of volunteers and regional directors. Due to the generous contributions of adoptive families and Beardie lovers, the program remains in good stead. No healthy Beardie need ever be homeless with this active group of dedicated people.

BEARDED COLLIE

The popularity of the Beardie has ensured that the majority of people nowadays have some idea of what the breed looks like. Gone are the days when you have to explain to everyone what a Bearded Collie is. However, due to its endearing appearance, the Bearded Collie may look appealing to many people who would not actually enjoy living with a Beardie should they acquire one. Thus it is essential to understand the characteristics of the breed before you choose it for your family. Once you have made your choice and obtained your puppy, you have many years ahead in which to be satisfied with or to rue your decision. Having said this, those of us who love these dogs do so for their many, many charms.

PHYSICAL CHARACTERISTICS

Beardies are medium-sized dogs, but they often seem much bigger due to their larger-than-life personalities. Although Beardies can seem quite small when curled up under a table, they become very large when jumping up at a friend in her best suit.

Males are much stronger in build and bulkier in coat than females, despite only a one- to two-inch difference in height at the shoulders. Consequently, males require substantially more of everything: more food, more grooming and often more strength in their owners' arms to control the leashes of their bouncy Beardie boys in adolescence.

One of the major physical attributes of the typical Bearded Collie is its lack of exaggeration and its consequent soundness of structure. Because Beardies are built along the lines of rather a basic dog shape, they probably are not as prone to some of the stresses and consequent structural weaknesses of some other breeds.

The movement of the Bearded Collie is, or should be, even, totally sound and smooth, with long-reaching strides and a fluid effect. This is a most beautiful feature of the breed. The head and expression are also most individual, with a broad, flat skull; muzzle that is equal in length to the area from the stop to the back of the skull; and inquiring, expressive eyes.

Another rather unusual aspect of the breed is the pigmentation. The nose and lip pigment follows the birth coloring, being black, blue, brown or fawn. The eyes

Beardies adore the company of well-behaved children. It is important to teach children and dogs to treat each other in a gentle manner.

should also tone with the coat coloring and change as the dog grows. In fact, the whole coloring of the dog is constantly changing through time and is a most interesting trait of the breed. For instance, the brown Beardie puppy is quite chocolate at eight weeks, only to change gradually to pale fawn, sometimes almost to white, by about 12 to 16 months. The coat may then darken gradually again until the full adult coat is gained by about four or five years of age. In the case of browns particularly,

IN LIVING COLOR

There are only four main coat colors in Bearded Collie puppies. Despite all of the adult shadings that occur, all Beardies are born either black, brown, blue or fawn, with or without (but usually with) white collie markings. All four colors may also come as tricolors, with additional tan markings on the cheeks, eyebrows, legs and under the tail. The pigmentation and eye coloring are determined by the color of the coat.

A young black and white Beardie, starting to feel at home in his new environment.

the constant growth of coat means that the color is always changing—throughout the dog's life and in different areas of the coat at any one time. At the same time, the eyes are constantly changing in color as well. Eyes can change from an almost yellow color in a youngster to perhaps a deep amber or copper in a mature dog. In this

way, the dog really provides an ever-changing level of attractiveness. Perhaps to a lesser degree, the other colors undergo the same changes. For example, the newborn's black will lighten and darken at similar times, probably never really to regain its original blackness. Blues will also lighten to nearly silver at around 12 to 16 months and then gradually regain much of their birth color by maturity. Born fawns are perhaps the least common of all the colors. Generally, although not always, they have a somewhat less attractive eye coloring, which can be rather pale. Additionally, there are more constraints on fawns in breeding; when choosing a mate, pigmentation and color are big considerations. Nonetheless, the fawn coat coloring is very lovely, being mushroom in hue in a baby and often having a frosting of white as the coat matures. A fawn with good eye coloring is a beautiful dog.

The Bearded Collie is a very attractive breed, capable of a most dramatic transformation from a scruffy, shaggy type to stylish show dog with comparatively little effort. Personally, I find this to be one of the breed's most endearing qualities.

THE GREAT ESCAPE

Many Beardies are highly skilled escape artists, being capable of scaling an 8-foot fence if they wish to. Others simply never consider this option at all and are happy to sit behind a 4-foot fence without ever once considering hopping over it. It is important that any area, such as your yard, in which your Beardie is to have unrestrained access, is properly secure for you to be safe rather than sorry.

PERSONALITY

Although hugely rewarding to so many families, the Bearded Collie would not be the easiest breed for some to live with. Beardies have strong and exuberant personalities. They are loving and giving dogs...and they are prepared to love and give at all times, whether you are of the same frame of mind or not. The typical Bearded Collie is not usually a one-person dog; it is a family dog.

Beardies are not suitable at all for people who cannot spend a lot of time with them. It would not be fair to leave a Beardie alone in the house all day while you go to work. Beardies need companionship and entertainment or they make their own fun (a.k.a. mischief). It is perfectly possible for a Beardie to dismantle a home if left without entertainment for long periods. Beardies find it impossible to curtail their natural *joie de vivre* simply at the will of their owners, despite the fact that they are intensely eager-to-please dogs. This breed is suited to the energetic, outdoor-loving owner, perhaps with children around the ages of, say, eight years and older. The whole family needs to be committed to the dog and to spending time with him.

Beardies find it extremely hard not to bounce, jumping up on you at the most inopportune times. Although with training their jumping up can be curtailed, I find it can never be wholly eradicated!

Beardies can have penetrating and, sometimes, excessive barking abilities. Please keep this in mind

if you have neighbors that might not appreciate hearing what your Beardie has to say!

Having said all this, many, many people adore the breed. Beardies are hugely rewarding and cheer you up when you are most down. They are very trainable and quick to learn basic obedience.

Beardie puppies love outdoor recreation, especially picnics with young friends.

WHAT'S THAT NOISE?

Bearded Collies have a highly developed sense of hearing and can become quite distressed by strangely pitched noises. Many Beardies are fearful of gunfire, jet planes or fireworks for this reason. The problem can become quite acute in the middle-aged dog who may be losing his hearing slightly; the dog seems unable to make sense of strange sudden noises. Later in life, perhaps as the dog loses more hearing, the problem often lessens.

PAW PADDING

The Bearded Collie should have coat between the pads of his feet. This helps to insulate the dog's feet when working in cold conditions.

Beardies are bright and attentive learners, but they can become bored quickly. Training sessions should be kept short and not too intense.

Beardies are generally excellent with children. This depends, of course, on the individual dog and also on the children in question. Children should always be expected to behave responsibly with dogs. No dog should be left unsupervised with young children, but, as dogs go, Beardies are generally considered to be one of the more suitable breeds for families with children. My own dogs took on my children, having not had any experience with babies for generations, with pride and devoted love. Beardies are often able to temper their exuberance, in a way they find totally impossible at other times, to a level suitable for children! Remember, though, that the Beardie is a herding dog and he may instinctively want to "herd" his "flock" of

The brown Bearded Collie is quite chocolate as a young puppy, but lightens and then darkens as the dog matures. This three-year-old brown male is in full adult coat.

small charges, which can include other pets as well, making supervision necessary.

It is important to encourage children not to treat the Bearded Collie as another child, something that may bring out the worst in a Beardie. The dog will often take the initiative and build upon the "child" game to excess, for instance, when playing chasing games. Beardies often have to be taught when to stop. Likewise, Beardies will sometimes pick up characteristics of other dogs and copy them, so don't let your Beardie have access to observing aggressive or unpleasant types in the dog world. As for other dogs, Beardies usually get along well with them, especially if raised with them.

Beardies need plenty of exercise and, once they are offered it, will generally insist upon it on a regular basis. Walks on the lead are fine but, in my opinion, an adult Beardie really needs lots of free running. As a Beardie owner, you must have a securely fenced yard or have access to another safe enclosure for off-leash exercise. Beardies are prepared to run endlessly, loving to chase balls or play with other dogs. I feel this is definitely the best and easiest way to exercise your Beardie and to keep him happy and healthy. The Beardie is not the type of dog to let you out of this exercise commitment in wet weather, so

be prepared with suitable all-weather gear.

Fortunately, the typical Beardie coat is ideally suited to all types of weather. The coat insulates against heat and protects the body against damp and cold, which can rarely penetrate the thick undercoat. An added advantage is that the coat sheds dirt, as the mud dries and the debris drops off, to leave a fairly clean dog and a rather dirty floor.

Born-black Bearded Collies will likely not retain the same darkness in the black parts of the coat in adulthood. This is a born-black male at seven months.

WATERPROOF DOG

A Bearded Collie may get soaking wet to the touch, but rarely gets wet right to the skin unless being bathed. This is due to the thick double coat, the fluffy undercoat acting as an insulating waterproof layer. For this reason, Beardies are ideally suited to work in all sorts of weather conditions.

With all of this energy and ability to bounce, the Beardie has a natural ability when it comes to agility competition. A lot of fun can be had with a Beardie and a supervised agility course. Remember that a young dog should be introduced gradually and that agility is more stressful on the dog's limbs than normal exercise. It is sensible to ask your veterinarian for an opinion about your dog's suitability for agility and a sensible age to begin training, probably around one year. As a precaution, most organizations do not permit dogs younger than 12 months old in agility competition.

HEALTH CONSIDERATIONS

Considering that the Bearded Collie was revived from near obscurity by Mrs. Willison's breedings involving very few dogs, all breed members today descend from a fairly narrow gene pool. At the time, Mrs. Willison had access to so few animals upon which to found not only her kennel but also, as it turned out, the whole future of the breed. These original dogs were registered by means of a judge authenticating the breeders' claims that the dogs were Bearded Collies. This method was phased out by England's Kennel Club in the

The Bearded Collie makes an excellent family dog, as he attaches himself to all members of the pack.

early 1970s, and so the option of bringing in further unregistered dogs, with the resultant input of fresh breeding, was no longer available.

Basically, all modern-day Bearded Collies could be considered to be quite closely linked genetically. Consequently, there is little scope for very close breeding in Bearded Collies, and close breeding naturally increases the chance of defects or faults occurring in the puppies.

There are various terms used in dog breeding. Linebreeding, the most commonly employed method of breeders, is drawing on one or more (hopefully superior) dogs in the background of a five-generation pedigree in an effort to obtain the dogs' best points and pass them on to the puppies. Close linebreeding might be a grandfather to granddaughter combination, for instance. Inbreeding, a method frowned

upon by some breeders, would be defined by persistent very close family breeding such as father/daughter, half-brother/half-sister or brother/sister, for instance. Dogs can also be inbred where the same ancestors repeatedly occur in the background of the pedigree.

Close family breeding should only be attempted with extreme care, if at all, in Bearded Collies. At all times, pedigrees are likely to carry some dogs a few times, but excessively close breeding can only increase the probability of defects appearing in the puppies. For this reason, breeding Bearded Collies should not be undertaken lightly and should be undertaken only by people with full knowledge of the backgrounds of the dogs in the pedigrees.

Having said this, Bearded Collies are blessed with remarkably few of the more well-known inherited defects that affect many breeds. There are, however, various conditions which, although not necessarily breed-specific,

The Bearded Collie is a natural born runner with great endurance. In modern times, this translates into a bouncy, happy dog that needs lots of exercise to stay fit in mind and body—and he enjoys exercising with a friend!

As a puppy, the Beardie is an energetic bundle that loves to play. In the canine play stance, this youngster is extending an invitation for you to join his game.

may be of interest to the prospective puppy owner, as they can occur in the Beardie.

HIP DYSPLASIA

This is a distressing condition affecting the hip joint. The hip is a ball-and-socket joint that may be affected by the socket's not being deep enough or the ball's being incorrectly formed, and thus a general laxity of the hip. Often, as a consequence, arthritic changes occur in the joint. This is a painful condition, and the dog will suffer lameness and pain if arthritis is present. It is possible to x-ray potential breeding stock for signs of this disease, and good breeders will do so. The x-rays, taken by a veterinarian, are sent to the Orthopedic Foundation for Animals (OFA) and evaluated by a panel of veterinarians according to a specified formulation. A grading system allows breeders to ascertain the health of their dogs'

Carefully socialize your Bearded Collie with all types of other creatures, not just dogs. This Beardie is safely getting acquainted with a rabbit. You must use caution with small pets and your exuberant Beardie.

hips and, if a dog is affected, to what degree. Dogs with any degree of dysplasia should not be bred, and dogs with healthy hips are assigned an OFA certification number.

Although there are affected dogs in the breed, we are fortunate that Beardies as a breed have relatively good hips. This is even more encouraging as many, many Beardies are routinely x-rayed. Different countries have differing methods of scoring, but one thing is certain: only Beardies with healthy hips should be bred. Prospective owners should ask the breeder for proof of the parents' hip clearances before buying a puppy. Even the greatest care by the breeder will not ensure that resultant puppies will grow up free from hip dysplasia, though, so a certain amount of risk is involved, as it is with the purchase of any dog.

UNILATERAL OR BILATERAL CRYPTORCHIDISM

In some male Bearded Collies, one or both of the testicles will fail to descend into the scrotum and will remain in the inguinal region or in the abdominal cavity. I find it should be possible to feel both testes in the male dog from an early age (six to eight weeks or less), although some experience will be necessary in checking males. If the testes cannot be felt at this age, I believe that there is a

Do You Know about Hip Dysplasia?

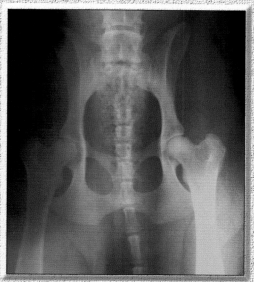

X-ray of a dog with "Good" hips.

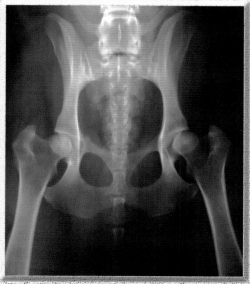

X-ray of a dog with "Moderate" dysplastic hips.

Hip dysplasia is a fairly common condition found in pure-bred dogs. When a dog has hip dysplasia, his hind leg has an incorrectly formed hip joint. By constant use of the hip joint, it becomes more and more loose, wears abnormally and may become arthritic.

Hip dysplasia can only be confirmed with an x-ray, but certain symptoms may indicate a problem. Your dog may have a hip dysplasia problem if he walks in a peculiar manner, hops instead of smoothly runs, uses his hind legs in unison (to keep the pressure off the weak joint), has trouble getting up from a prone position or always sits with both legs together on one side of his body.

As the dog matures, he may adapt well to life with a bad hip, but in a few years the arthritis develops and many dogs with hip dysplasia become crippled.

Hip dysplasia is considered an inherited disease and only can be diagnosed definitively by x-ray when the dog is two years old, although symptoms often appear earlier. Some experts claim that a special diet might help your puppy outgrow the bad hip, but the usual treatments are surgical. The removal of the pectineus muscle, the removal of the round part of the femur, reconstructing the pelvis and replacing the hip with an artificial one are all surgical interventions that are expensive, but they are usually very successful. Follow the advice of your veterinarian.

Beardies make excellent partners for ballroom dancing, especially for partners that are their own height.

high chance that the dog will not be "entire" at maturity. Beardie males should normally have both testes fully descended into the scrotum by, at the latest, around six months of age, although it is possible for this to occur later. If one or both of the testes remain in the abdominal cavity, the dog is termed unilaterally or bilaterally cryptorchid (the term *cryptos* meaning "hidden"). Your veterinarian will probably advise neutering the dog, as testicular cancer is more common in these dogs since the testicle(s) can reach an abnormally high temperature inside the body. It is possible for a male Beardie with only one descended testicle to sire a litter;

however, these dogs should *not* be used at stud, as the condition is often inherited.

UMBILICAL HERNIAS
These are formed at the site of the attachment of the umbilical cord to the puppy. A weakness of the abdominal wall allows the protrusion of a small amount of tissue under the skin. This is not an uncommon problem and can occur in any breed. Small umbilical hernias rarely cause a problem for the dog. Some veterinarians may advocate the repair of a small hernia, which involves a relatively simple procedure under anesthesia. Larger hernias are more serious and definitely require repair. Occasionally the hernia will

ADDITIONAL CONCERNS

In addition to the issues mentioned, there are other diseases that have been reported in the Beardie, including hereditary eye disease, various types of allergies, cancer, hypothyroidism and auto-immune problems. Further, a study to find the mode of inheritance for Addison's disease (an adrenal-gland disorder) in the Beardie is under way. A good breeder will speak honestly to you about any health problems that have occurred in his line and will have ensured as thoroughly as possible the hereditary health of all breeding stock through appropriate testing and certification.

involve the abdominal contents (covered externally with skin). In this instance, the puppy should have had effective repair and recovery while still with the breeder. The condition is generally considered to be inherited, and dogs affected to any but the most minor degree are, therefore, really not suitable for breeding.

MOUTHS

Over recent years, many breeders have noticed an increasing problem with mouths in the breed. A Bearded Collie should have a scissor bite; that is, the upper incisors closely overlap the lower incisors. Adult dogs should possess the correct bite, and many puppies will have this bite by the time they leave the breeder. Some will have a slightly overshot bite (the top incisors overlapping the bottom incisors with a gap between the two sets of teeth), but very often a slightly overshot bite will correct with age and is a normal aspect of puppy growth. However, some overshot mouths appear not to correct with maturity. An increasing number of dogs have rather narrow bottom jaws, which results in the lower canine teeth's grazing, or protruding into, the tissue of the upper

gums. This condition may improve with age; if not, the problem canine teeth can be removed by a veterinarian. Although not an ideal situation at all, the procedure is necessary and relatively simple. Dogs requiring this treatment are not suitable for showing or breeding. Hopefully this problem will be corrected by breeders' only selecting dogs who have had perfect mouths since puppyhood for their breeding programs.

Bearded Collies are loving and giving dogs, enjoying snuggle time just as much as playtime.

Beardies are very devoted to their owners and like to accompany them wherever they go.

BEARDED COLLIE

The standard of any breed is the description of the ideal dog of that breed. All typical specimens of the Bearded Collie will have many attributes described in the standard; the best Bearded Collies, in show terms, will be those that conform the most closely to the standard in all respects. Having said this, the standard has to be interpreted. In this lies the potential variation—since the interpreters of the standard are people, they will often see the dog in differing guises!

I thought, when I was a 13-year-old child, that my first Bearded Collie adhered remarkably closely to the breed standard, so much so that I felt she couldn't fail to win Best in Show at any show we entered. In fact she was not, in show terms, one of the world's best Beardies (although she did end up as grandmother of one of my first champions). Even if judges had been foolish enough to see her as I did, they rarely had a chance to, since she invariably left the ring as we ran around it, with me in compulsory attendance!

Nevertheless, experienced and knowledgeable judges are used to reading and interpreting standards and do so regularly in order to obtain a consistent blueprint by which to judge the breed. The breed standard is also very important for breeders as they assess which dogs should be bred.

THE AMERICAN KENNEL CLUB STANDARD FOR THE BEARDED COLLIE

Characteristics: The Bearded Collie is hardy and active, with an aura of strength and agility characteristic of a real working dog. Bred for centuries as a companion and servant of man, the Bearded Collie is a devoted and intelligent member of the family. He is stable and self-confident, showing no signs of shyness or aggression.

The Bearded Collie's coat is straight and shaggy. The coat is a natural one, not trimmed for the show ring.

This is a natural and unspoiled breed.

General Appearance: The Bearded Collie is a medium sized dog with a medium length coat that follows the natural lines of the body and allows plenty of daylight under the body. The body is long and lean, and, though strongly made, does not appear heavy. A bright inquiring expression is a distinctive feature of the breed. The Bearded Collie should be shown in a natural stance.

Head: The head is in proportion to the size of the dog. The skull is broad and flat; the stop is moderate; the cheeks are well filled beneath the eyes; the muzzle is strong and full; the foreface is equal in length to the distance between the stop and occiput. The nose is large and squarish. A snipy muzzle is to be penalized. (See Color section for pigmentation.) *Eyes:* The eyes are large, expressive, soft and affectionate, but not round nor protruding, and are set widely apart. The eyebrows are arched to the sides to frame the eyes and are long enough to blend smoothly into the coat on the sides of the head. (See Color section for eye color.) *Ears:* The ears are medium sized, hanging and covered with long hair. They are set level with the eyes. When the dog is alert, the ears have a slight lift at the base.

Teeth: The teeth are strong and white, meeting in a scissors bite. Full dentition is desirable.

Neck: The neck is in proportion to the length of the body, strong and slightly arched, blending smoothly into the shoulders.

Forequarters: The shoulders are well laid back at an angle of approximately 45°; a line drawn from the highest point of the shoulder blade to the forward point of articulation approximates a right angle with a line from the forward point of articulation to the point of the elbow. The tops of the shoulder blades lie in against the withers, but they slope outwards from there sufficiently to accommodate the desired spring of ribs. The legs are straight and vertical, with substantial, but not heavy, bone and are covered with shaggy hair all around. The pasterns are flexible without weakness.

Body: The body is longer than it is high in an approximate ratio of five to four, length measured from point of chest to point of buttocks, height measured at the highest point of the withers. The length of the back comes from the length of the ribcage and not that of the loin. The back is level. The ribs are well sprung from the spine but are flat at the sides. The chest is deep, reaching at least to the elbows. The loins are strong. The level back line blends smoothly into the curve of the rump. A flat croup or a steep croup is to be severely penalized.

Hindquarters: The hind legs are powerful and muscular at the thighs with well bent stifles. The hocks are low. In normal stance, the bones below the hocks are perpendicular to the ground and parallel to each other when viewed from the rear; the hind feet fall just behind a perpendicular line from the point of buttocks when viewed from the side. The legs are covered with shaggy hair all around. *Tail:* The tail is set low and is long enough for the end of the bone to reach at least the point of the hocks. It is normally carried low with an upward swirl at the tip while the dog is standing. When the dog is excited or in motion, the curve is accentuated and the tail may be raised but is never carried beyond a vertical line. The tail is covered with abundant hair.

Feet: The feet are oval in shape with the soles well padded. The toes are arched and close together, and well covered with hair including between the pads.

Coat: The coat is double with the undercoat soft, furry and close. The outercoat is flat, harsh, strong and shaggy, free from wooliness and curl, although a slight wave is permissible. The coat falls naturally to either side but must never be artificially parted. The length and density of the hair are sufficient to provide a protective coat and to enhance the shape of the dog, but not so profuse as to obscure the natural lines of the body. The dog should be shown as naturally as is consistent with good grooming but the coat must not be trimmed in any way. On the head, the bridge of the nose is sparsely covered with hair which is slightly longer on the sides to cover the lips. From the cheeks, the lower lips and under the chin, the coat increases in length towards the chest, forming the typical beard. An excessively long, silky coat or one which has been trimmed in any way must be severely penalized.

Color: *Coat:* All Bearded Collies are born either black, blue, brown or fawn, with or without white markings. With maturity, the coat color may lighten, so that a born black may become any shade of gray from black to slate to silver, a born brown from chocolate to sandy. Blues and fawns also show shades from dark to light. Where white occurs, it only appears on the foreface as a blaze, on the skull, on the tip of the tail, on the chest, legs and feet and around the neck. The white hair does not grow on the body behind the shoulder nor on the face to surround the eyes. Tan markings occasionally appear and are acceptable on the eyebrows, inside the ears, on the cheeks, under the root of the tail, and on the legs where the white joins the main color. *Pigmentation:* Pigmentation on the Bearded Collie follows coat color. In a born black, the eye rims, nose and lips are black, whereas in the born blue, the pigmentation is a blue-gray color. A born brown dog has brown pigmentation and born fawns a correspondingly lighter brown. The pigmentation is completely filled in and shows no sign of spots. *Eyes:* Eye color will generally tone with the coat color. In a born blue or fawn, the distinctively lighter eyes are correct and must not be penalized.

Size: The ideal height at the withers is 21–22 inches for adult dogs and 20–21 inches for adult bitches. Height over and under the ideal is to be severely penalized. The express objective of this criterion is to insure that the Bearded Collie remains a medium sized dog.

Gait: Movement is free, supple and powerful. Balance combines good reach in forequarters with

Example of correct coloring.

Incorrect coloring. Patched white markings.

Incorrect coloring.
White extends beyond the shoulder line and around the eyes.

Correct tail.   Incorrect tail; set too high and curled.

strong drive in hindquarters. The back remains firm and level. The feet are lifted only enough to clear the ground, giving the impression that the dog glides along making minimum contact. Movement is lithe and flexible to enable the dog to make the sharp turns and sudden stops required of the sheepdog. When viewed from the front and rear, the front and rear legs travel in the same plane from the shoulder and hip joint to pads at all speeds. Legs remain straight, but feet move inward as speed increases until the edges of the feet converge on a center line at a fast trot.

Serious Faults:
- Snipy muzzle
- Flat croup or steep croup
- Excessively long, silky coat
- Trimmed or sculptured coat
- Height over or under the ideal

Approved August 9, 1978

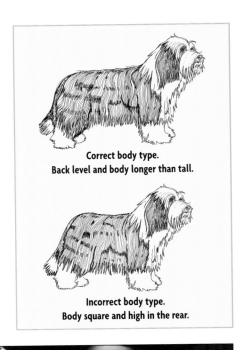

Correct body type.
Back level and body longer than tall.

Incorrect body type.
Body square and high in the rear.

This Bearded Collie did very well at Crufts, the biggest show in the breed's homeland. A proud owner shows off her champion.

How the dam of your puppy measures up to the standard will be a fair indication of how well your puppy will conform. Quality begets quality, thus it is important to see the dam and sire, if possible, of your puppy before making your selection.

BEARDED COLLIE

Once you have chosen your breed, you need to choose a breeder. It is vital that you obtain your puppy from a reputable source. Although one can never provide an absolute guarantee with a puppy, a reputable breeder will have done everything possible to ensure that the puppy you buy will be a happy, healthy addition to your family. Reputable breeders will have any necessary tests performed on their breeding stock to ensure, as far as they can, that the dogs do not have any hereditary defects. Although Beardies are generally free of many proven problems, good breeders will x-ray their breeding stock for hip dysplasia and screen for hereditary eye disease.

Once you have located a suitable breeder, go and see their dogs and discuss the breed with them. Be prepared for them to paint an honest picture of the breed and listen to what they say. They know the Beardie and will have a good idea if it is or is not the right breed for you.

Be honest—don't tell a breeder that you will want to show your dog if you have no intention of doing so. It is unfair to try to buy a show prospect and never enter him in any shows. Breeders who show their dogs like to see them in the show ring. Most puppies in the litter will look the same to you, regardless of their show potential, and they will certainly make just as nice family companions. Likewise, the breeder has a responsibility to tell you if the puppy has

FINDING A QUALIFIED BREEDER
Before you begin your puppy search, ask your veterinarian, other owners and breeders to refer you to someone they believe is reputable. Responsible breeders usually raise only one or two breeds of dog. Avoid any breeder who has several different breeds or has several litters at the same time. Dedicated breeders are usually involved with a breed or other dog club. Many participate in some sport or activity related to their breed. Just as you want to be assured of the breeder's qualifications, the breeder wants to be assured that you will make a worthy owner. Expect the breeder to interview you, asking questions about your goals for the pup, your experience with dogs and what kind of home you will provide.

some aspect (usually termed a show fault) that would render the dog unsuitable for entering a show. For instance, mismarking, like too much white or white markings in an unacceptable place, e.g., on the back or on the outer thighs of the dog, would be considered a fault in the show ring but have no effect on the dog as a pet.

This newborn Bearded Collie pup has not even opened his eyes yet.

If you have a particular feeling for one color only, you should stipulate this, since you should be living with the dog for many years and want to be totally satisfied with your choice. However, don't forget that the coat color is going to change a lot over those years.

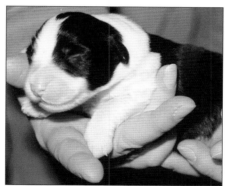

Most breeders will not show you their puppies until they are at least five or six weeks of age. This baby is only a few days old and is not ready to be exposed to strange people or other dogs.

Once the litter is born, try to get to see the puppies at a fairly young age. Most breeders will be happy to show you the puppies after around five to six weeks of age, once they have begun to be weaned from the dam. It would not be sensible for you to make a definite choice at this stage, since the pups change so much and their temperaments cannot be assessed at such a young age.

When it comes time to choose your puppy, be guided by the breeder. He will have experience in puppy matchmaking, especially in evaluating individual temperaments in relation to prospective owners. A lot of people are attracted to the puppy that is the first to approach them, but so much depends on which puppy had just been sleeping or which

When you go to meet the litter, you must observe the dam as well. She should be a healthy, sound representative of the breed.

one had been playing hard just before you arrived to see them.

With regard to physical characterics, don't forget that these will alter with age and growth. The smallest puppy in the litter may turn out to be the biggest adult, for instance. Puppies invariably carry their tails up, sometimes over the back, but frequently the highest carried tail will be carried correctly at maturity. Also, always check the bite of your selected puppy to be sure that it is neither overshot nor undershot. If you have a definite preference, though, among the puppies available, discuss this specific puppy with the breeder and get his opinion on how the pup will mature.

SELECTING FROM THE LITTER

Before you visit a litter of puppies, promise yourself that you won't fall for the first pretty face you see! Decide on your goals for your puppy—show prospect, herding dog, obedience or agility competitor, family companion—and then look for a puppy who displays the appropriate qualities. In most litters, there is an Alpha pup (the bossy puppy), and occasionally a shy fellow who is less confident, with the rest of the litter falling somewhere in the middle. "Middle-of-the-roaders" are safe bets for most families and novice competitors.

You will normally be provided with a full diet sheet, worming and inoculation history, information on insurance, the pedigree, documentation on registration and a sales contract with some type of health guarantee and after-sale support. Most breeders would much prefer you to contact them with any worries or questions and will also be happy for you to return with the puppy for grooming advice as he grows. You also should see the parents' health documentation, which should include certification from the Orthopedic Foundation for Animals (OFA) and the Canine Eye Registration Foundation (CERF).

WHERE TO BEGIN?
You are convinced that the Bearded Collie is the ideal dog for you, so how do you find a reputable breeder? You should inquire about breeders in your area who enjoy a good reputation in the breed. The best way to do this is to contact the AKC-recognized national club for the breed, the Bearded Collie Club of America (http://beardie.net/bcca), and search for regional clubs and member breeders. BCCA breeders are obliged to follow a code of ethics, which can be viewed on the club's website. You are looking for an established breeder with outstanding dog ethics and a strong commitment to the breed. New owners should have as many

You should select a puppy with clear, bright, healthy eyes, sparkling with puppy curiosity.

questions as they have doubts. An established breeder is indeed the one to answer your four million questions and make you comfortable with your choice of the Bearded Collie. An established breeder will sell you a puppy at a fair price if, and only if, the breeder determines that you are a suitable, worthy owner of this breed and of his dogs. An established breeder can be relied upon for advice at any reasonable time. A reputable breeder will accept a puppy back, sometimes without penalty, should you decide that this not the right dog for you.

When choosing a breeder, reputation is much more important than convenience of location. Do not be overly impressed by breeders who run brag advertisements in the presses about their stupendous lines. The real quality

THE FAMILY TREE

Your puppy's pedigree is his family tree. Just as a child may resemble his parents and grandparents, so too will a puppy reflect the qualities, good and bad, of his ancestors, especially those in the first two generations. Therefore, it's important to know as much as possible about a puppy's immediate relatives. Reputable and experienced breeders should be able to explain the pedigree and why they chose to breed from the particular dogs they used.

breeders are quiet and unassuming. You hear about them at dog shows and by word of mouth. You may be well advised to avoid the novice who lives only a couple of miles away. The local novice breeder, trying so hard to get rid of that first litter of puppies, is more than accommodating and

anxious to sell you one. That breeder will charge you as much as any established breeder, but the novice breeder isn't going to interrogate you and your family about your intentions with the puppy, the environment and training you can provide, etc. That breeder will be nowhere to be found when your poorly bred, badly adjusted four-pawed monster starts to growl, pick fights with the cat and generally become unruly.

Choosing the right breeder is an important first step in dog ownership. Fortunately, the majority of Bearded Collie breeders are devoted to the breed and its well-being. New owners should have little problem finding a reputable breeder who doesn't live on the other side of the country. The Bearded Collie Club of America can help you find reputable breeders in your state or region of the country. Potential owners are encouraged to go to dog shows to see Bearded Collies in action, to meet the handlers firsthand and to get an idea of what Bearded Collies look like outside a photographer's lens. Provided you approach the handlers when they are not busy with the dogs, most are more than willing to answer questions, recommend breeders and give advice.

Once you have contacted and met a breeder or two and made your choice about which breeder is best suited to your needs, it's

PEDIGREE VS. REGISTRATION CERTIFICATE

Too often new owners are confused between these two important documents. Your puppy's pedigree, essentially a family tree, is a written record of a dog's genealogy of three generations or more. The pedigree will show you the names as well as performance titles of all dogs in your pup's background. Your breeder must provide you with a registration application, with his part properly filled out. You must complete the application and send it to the AKC with the proper fee. Every puppy must come from a litter that has been AKC-registered by the breeder, born in the US and from a sire and dam that are also registered with the AKC.

The seller must provide you with complete records to identify the puppy. The AKC requires that the seller provide the buyer with the following: breed; sex, color and markings; date of birth; litter number (when available); names and registration numbers of the parents; breeder's name; and date sold or delivered.

time to visit the litter. Keep in mind that many top breeders have waiting lists. Sometimes new owners have to wait a year or longer for a puppy. If you are really committed to the breeder whom you've selected, then you will wait (and hope for an early arrival!). If not, you may have to go with your second- or third-choice breeder. Don't be too anxious, however. If the breeder doesn't have any waiting list or any customers, there is probably a good reason. It's no different from visiting a restaurant with no clientele. The better establishments have waiting lists—and it's usually worth the wait!

PUPPY PARASITES

Parasites are nasty little critters that live in or on your dog or puppy. Most puppies are born with ascarid roundworms, which are acquired from dormant ascarids residing in the dam. Other parasites can be acquired through contact with infected fecal matter. Take a stool sample to your vet for testing. He will prescribe a safe wormer to treat any parasites found in your puppy's stool. Always have a fecal test performed at your puppy's annual veterinary exam.

Since you are likely to be choosing a Bearded Collie as a pet dog and not a show dog or work-

With such an adorable bunch, it would be hard to select just one! You will need the help of an experienced breeder to pick your perfect match.

possess the typical physical and
temperament traits of the breed,
individual personality varies from
pup to pup. Beware of the shy or
overly aggressive puppy, and be
especially conscious of the
nervous Bearded Collie pup.

If you have intentions of
having your new charge herding
sheep, there are many more
considerations. The parents of a
future working dog should have
excellent qualifications, including actual work experience as
well as herding titles in their
pedigrees.

ing herder, you simply should
select a pup that is friendly,
healthy, sound and attractive.
While a well-bred Beardie should

The physical
characteristics of
the Bearded Collie
will change with
age. One example
is the coat—look at
the difference
between the puppy
coat and adult
coat.

The sex of your puppy is largely a matter of personal taste and which pup's personality appeals to you. Both sexes are playful and loving. Pet Beardies of either sex should be spayed (females) or neutered (males), as this has important health benefits and can diminish some sex-related behaviors seen in unaltered dogs.

Breeders commonly allow visitors to see the litter after the fifth or sixth week, and puppies

GETTING ACQUAINTED

When visiting a litter, ask the breeder for suggestions on how best to interact with the puppies. If possible, get right into the middle of the pack and sit down with them. Observe which pups climb into your lap and which ones shy away. Toss a toy for them to chase and bring back to you. It's easy to fall in love with the puppy who picks you, but keep your future objectives in mind before you make your final decision.

Bring the whole family along when choosing a Bearded Collie. The Beardie is a family dog, so everyone should take part in the decision.

Part of helping your Bearded Collie settle into his new home is to acclimate him to his crate, which will be his own personal den.

leave for their new homes between the eighth and tenth week. Breeders who permit their puppies to leave early are more interested in a profit than in their puppies' well-being. Puppies need to learn the rules of the trade from their dams, and most dams continue teaching the pups manners and dos and don'ts until at least the eighth week. Breeders spend significant amounts of time with the Bearded Collie toddlers so that they are able to interact with the "other species," i.e., humans. Given the long history that dogs and humans have, bonding between the two species is natural but must be nurtured. A well-bred, well-socialized Bearded Collie pup wants nothing more than to be near you and please you.

A COMMITTED NEW OWNER
By now you should understand what makes the Bearded Collie a most unique and special dog, one that may fit nicely into your family and lifestyle. If you have researched breeders, you should be able to recognize a knowledgeable and responsible Bearded Collie breeder who cares not only about his pups but also about what kind of owner you will be. If you have completed the final step in your new journey, you have found a litter, or possibly two, of quality Bearded Collie pups.

A visit with the puppies and their breeder should be an education in itself. Breed research, breeder selection and puppy visitation are very important aspects of finding the puppy of your dreams. Beyond that, these things also lay the foundation for a successful future with your pup. Puppy personalities within each litter vary, from the shy and easygoing puppy to the one who is dominant and assertive, with most pups falling somewhere in between. By spending time with the puppies, you will be able to recognize certain behaviors and what these behaviors indicate about each pup's temperament. Which type of pup will complement your family dynamics is best determined by observing the puppies in action within their "pack." Your breeder's expertise and recommendations are also valuable. Although you may fall in love with a bold and brassy male, the breeder may suggest that another pup would be best for you. The breeder's experience in rearing Bearded Collie pups and matching their tempera-ments with appropriate humans offers the best assurance that your pup will meet your needs and expectations. The type of puppy that you select is just as important as your decision that the Bearded Collie is the breed for you.

The decision to live with a Bearded Collie is a serious commitment and not one to be taken lightly. This puppy is a living sentient being that will be dependent on you for basic survival for his entire life. Beyond the basics of survival—food, water, shelter and protection—he needs much, much more. The new pup needs love, nurturing

Your Bearded Collie puppy will be alert, energetic and curious, likely with a dash of puppy mischief.

and a proper canine education to mold him into a responsible, well-behaved canine citizen. Your Bearded Collie's health and good manners will need consistent monitoring and regular "tune-ups," so your job as a responsible dog owner will be ongoing throughout every stage of his life. If you are not prepared to accept these responsibilities and commit

Stimulate your puppy with a variety of toys to keep his mind busy and to limit his mischief-making.

to them for at least the next decade, likely longer, then you are not prepared to own a dog of any breed.

Although the responsibilities of owning a dog may at times tax your patience, the joy of living with your Bearded Collie far outweighs the workload, and a well-mannered adult dog is worth your time and effort. Before your very eyes, your new charge will grow up to be your most loyal friend, devoted to his family unconditionally.

YOUR BEARDED COLLIE SHOPPING LIST

Just as expectant parents prepare a nursery for their baby, so should you ready your home for the arrival of your Bearded Collie pup. If you have the necessary puppy supplies purchased and in place before he comes home, it will ease the puppy's transition from the warmth and familiarity of his mom and littermates to the brand-new environment of his new home and human family. You will be too busy to stock up and prepare your house after your pup comes home—that's for sure! Imagine how a pup must feel upon being transported to a strange new place. It's up to you to comfort him and to let your little pup know that he is going to be happy with you.

FOOD AND WATER BOWLS

Your puppy will need separate bowls for his food and water. Stainless steel bowls are generally

COST OF OWNERSHIP
The purchase price of your puppy is merely the first expense in the typical dog budget. Quality dog food, veterinary care (sickness and health maintenance), dog supplies and grooming costs will add up to big bucks every year. Can you adequately afford to support a canine addition to the family?

preferred over plastic bowls since they sterilize better and pups are less inclined to chew on the metal. Heavy-duty ceramic bowls are popular, but consider how often you will have to pick up those heavy bowls. Buy adult-sized bowls, as your puppy will grow into them quickly.

THE DOG CRATE

If you think that crates are tools of punishment and confinement for when a dog has misbehaved, think again. Most breeders and almost all trainers recommend a crate as the preferred house-training aid as well as for all-around puppy training and safety. Because dogs are natural den creatures that prefer cave-like environments, the benefits of crate use are many. The crate provides the puppy with his very own "safe house," a cozy place to sleep, take a break or seek comfort with a favorite toy; a travel aid to house your dog when on the road, at motels or at the vet's office; a training aid to help teach your puppy proper toileting habits; a place of solitude when non-dog people happen to drop by and don't want a lively puppy—or even a well-behaved adult dog—saying hello or begging for their attention.

Crates come in several types, although the wire crate and the fiberglass airline-type crate are the most popular. Both are safe and

The crate is a helpful tool both indoors and out. Once your pup is accustomed to his crate, he will feel comfortable in it whenever you need to safely confine him.

your puppy will adjust to either one, so the choice is up to you. The wire crates offer better visibility for the pup as well as better ventilation and are more common for use in the home. Many of the wire crates easily collapse into suitcase-sized carriers. The fiberglass crates, similar to those used by the airlines for animal transport, are sturdier and more den-like. However, the fiberglass crates do not collapse and are less ventilated than a wire crate, which can be problematic in hot weather. These are used more often for travel. Some of the newer crates are made of heavy plastic mesh;

they are very lightweight and fold up into slim-line suitcases. However, a mesh crate might not be suitable for a pup with manic chewing habits.

Don't bother with a puppy-sized crate. Although your Bearded Collie will be a wee fellow when you bring him home, he will grow up in the blink of an eye and your puppy crate will be useless. It is better to get a crate that will accommodate your dog both as a pup and at full size. A large-sized crate will be necessary for a full-grown Bearded Collie, who stands approximately 22 inches high at the shoulder. A suggested crate size is 42 inches long by 28 inches wide by 32 inches high.

The temperament of a Bearded Collie, being that it is a bouncy, sociable dog, does not lend itself to long periods of confinement. Therefore, periods spent in the dog crate should always be short so that the dog sees the crate as a place of relaxation and not of restriction. Puppies, and adult dogs as well, should never be left in their crates needing to relieve themselves, as it is not suitable for a dog to be expected to stay in a crate "holding on" to a full bladder.

BEDDING AND CRATE PADS
Your puppy will enjoy some type of soft bedding in his "room" (the crate), something he can snuggle

CRATE EXPECTATIONS
To make the crate more inviting to your puppy, you can offer his first meal or two inside the crate, always keeping the crate door open so that he does not feel confined. Keep a favorite toy or two in the crate for him to play with while inside. You can also cover the crate at night with a lightweight sheet to make it more den-like and remove the stimuli of household activity. Never put him into his crate as punishment or as you are scolding him, since he will then associate his crate with negative situations and avoid going there.

This pampered pup enjoys the comforts of home, even outdoors!

CONFINEMENT

It is wise to keep your puppy confined to a small "puppy-proofed" area of the house for his first few weeks at home. Gate or block off a space near the door he will use for outdoor potty trips. Expandable baby gates are useful to create puppy's designated area. If he is allowed to roam through the entire house or even only several rooms, it will be more difficult to house-train him.

into to feel cozy and secure. Old towels or blankets are good choices for a young pup, since he may (and probably will) have a toileting accident or two in the crate or decide to chew on the bedding material. Once he is fully trained and out of the early chewing stage, you can replace the puppy bedding with a permanent crate pad if you prefer. Crate pads and other dog beds run the gamut from inexpensive to high-end

TOYS 'R SAFE

The vast array of tantalizing puppy toys is staggering. Stroll through any pet shop or pet-supply outlet and you will see that the choices can be overwhelming. However, not all dog toys are safe or sensible. Most very young puppies enjoy soft woolly toys that they can snuggle with and carry around. (You know they have outgrown them when they shred them up!) Avoid toys that have buttons, tabs or other enhancements that can be chewed off and swallowed. Soft toys and squeaky toys are fun, but you must remove them at the first sign of their being damaged or worn. Toys that rattle or make noise can excite a puppy, but they present the same danger as the squeaky kind and so require supervision. Hard rubber toys that bounce can also entertain a pup, but make sure that the toy is too big for your pup to swallow.

doggie-designer styles, but don't splurge on the good stuff until you are sure that your puppy is reliable and won't tear it up or make a mess on it.

PUPPY TOYS

Just as infants and older children require objects to stimulate their minds and bodies, puppies need toys to entertain their curious brains, wiggly paws and achy teeth. A fun array of safe doggie toys will help satisfy your puppy's chewing instincts and distract him from gnawing on the leg of your antique chair or your new leather sofa. Most puppy toys are cute and look as if they would be a lot of fun, but not all are necessarily safe or good for your puppy, so use caution when you go puppy-toy shopping.

Bearded Collie puppies are fairly aggressive chewers and only hard, strong, safe toys should be offered to them. The best "chewci-fiers" are sturdy nylon and hard rubber bones, which are safe to gnaw on and come in sizes appropriate for all age groups and breeds. Be especially careful of natural bones, which can splinter or develop dangerous sharp edges; pups can easily swallow or choke on those bone splinters. Veterinarians often tell of surgical nightmares involving bits of splintered bone, because, in addition to the danger of choking, the sharp pieces can damage the intestinal tract.

Similarly, rawhide chews, while a favorite of most dogs and puppies, can be equally dangerous. Pieces of rawhide are easily swallowed after they get soft and gummy from chewing, and dogs have been known to choke on large pieces of ingested rawhide. Rawhide chews should be offered only when you can supervise the puppy.

Soft woolly toys are special puppy favorites, particularly during teething, as it feels good to sink their aching teeth and gums into something soft. They come in a wide variety of cute shapes and sizes; some look like little stuffed animals. Puppies love to shake them up and toss them about or simply carry them around. Be careful of fuzzy toys that have button eyes or noses that your pup could chew off and swallow, and make sure that he does not disembowel a squeaky toy to remove the squeaker! Braided rope toys are similar in that they are fun to chew and toss around, but they shred easily and the strings are easy to swallow. The strings are not digestible and, if the puppy doesn't pass them in his stool, he could end up at the vet's office. As with rawhides, your puppy should be closely monitored with rope toys.

If you believe that your pup has ingested a piece of one of his toys, check his stools for the next

TEETHING TIME

All puppies chew. It's normal canine behavior. Chewing just plain feels good to a puppy, especially during the three- to five-month teething period when the adult teeth are breaking through the gums. Rather than attempting to eliminate such a strong natural chewing instinct, you will be more successful if you redirect it and teach your puppy what he may or may not chew. Correct inappropriate chewing with a sharp "No!" and offer him a chew toy, praising him when he takes it. Don't become discouraged. Chewing usually decreases after the adult teeth have come in.

couple of days to see if he passes the item when he defecates. At the same time, also watch for signs of intestinal distress. A call to your veterinarian might be in

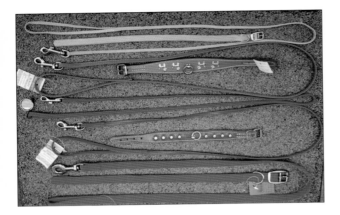

An everyday buckle collar is needed to attach identification tags, and a nylon lead is best for walking your new Bearded Collie pup.

order to get his advice and be on the safe side.

An all-time favorite toy for puppies (young and old!) is the empty gallon milk jug. Hard plastic juice containers—46 ounces or more—are also excellent. Such containers make lots of noise when they are batted about, and puppies go crazy with delight as they play with them. However, they don't often last very long, so be sure to remove and replace them when they get chewed up.

A word of caution about homemade toys: be careful with your choices of non-traditional play objects. Never use old shoes or socks, since a puppy cannot distinguish between the old ones on which he's allowed to chew and the new ones in your closet that are strictly off limits. That principle applies to anything that resembles something that you don't want your puppy to chew.

COLLARS

A lightweight nylon collar is the best choice for a very young pup. Quick-clip collars are easy to put on and remove, and they can be adjusted as the puppy grows. Introduce him to his collar as soon as he comes home to get him accustomed to wearing it. He'll get used to it quickly and won't mind a bit. Make sure that it is snug enough that it won't slip off, yet loose enough to be comfortable for the pup. You should be able to slip two fingers between the collar and his neck. Check the collar often, as puppies grow in spurts, and his collar can become too tight almost overnight.

LEASHES

A 6-foot nylon lead is an excellent choice for a young puppy. It is lightweight and not as tempting to chew as a leather lead. You can switch to a 6-foot leather lead after your pup has grown and is used to walking politely on a lead. For initial puppy walks and house-training purposes, you should invest in a shorter lead so that you have more control over the puppy. At first, you don't want him wandering too far away from you, and, when taking him out for toileting, you will want to keep him in the specific area chosen for his potty spot.

Once the puppy is heel-trained with a traditional leash, you can consider purchasing a

COLLARING OUR CANINES

The standard flat collar with a buckle or a snap, in leather, nylon or cotton, is widely regarded as the everyday all-purpose collar. If the collar fits correctly, you should be able to fit two fingers between the collar and the dog's neck.

Leather Buckle Collars

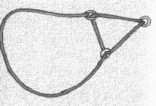

Limited-Slip Collar

The martingale, Greyhound or limited-slip collar is preferred by many dog owners and trainers. It is fixed with an extra loop that tightens when pressure is applied to the leash. The martingale collar gets tighter but does not "choke" the dog. The limited-slip collar should only be used for walking and training, not for free play or interaction with another dog. These types of collar should never be left on the dog, as the extra loop can lead to accidents.

Choke collars, usually made of stainless steel, are made for training purposes though are not recommended for small dogs or heavily coated breeds like the Beardie. The chains can injure small dogs or damage long/abundant coats. Thin nylon choke leads are commonly used on show dogs while in the ring, though they are not practical for everyday use.

Snap Bolt Choke Collar

The harness, with two or three straps that attach over the dog's shoulders and around his torso, is a humane and safe alternative to the conventional collar. By and large, a well-made harness is virtually escape-proof. Harnesses are available in nylon and mesh and can be outfitted on most dogs, with chest girths ranging from 10 to 30 inches.

Harness

Nylon Collar

Quick-Click Closure

Snake Chain

Chrome Steel

Fur-Saver

Choke Chain Collars

A head collar, composed of a nylon strap that goes around the dog's muzzle and a second strap that wraps around his neck, offers the owner better control over his dog. This device is recommended for problem-solving with dogs (including jumping up, pulling and aggressive behaviors) but must be used with care.

A training halter, including a flat collar and two straps made of nylon and webbing, is designed for walking. There are several on the market; some are more difficult to put on the dog than others. The halter harness, with two small slip rings at each end, is recommended for ease of use.

retractable lead. This type of lead is excellent for walking adult dogs that are already leash-wise. The retractable lead allows the dog to roam farther away from you and explore a wider area when out walking and also retracts when you need to keep him close to you. These leads come in different lengths and strengths for different sizes of dog.

HOME SAFETY FOR YOUR PUPPY

The importance of puppy-proofing cannot be overstated. In addition to making your house comfortable for your Bearded Collie's arrival, you also must make sure that your house is safe for your puppy before you bring him home. There are countless hazards in the owner's personal living environment that a pup can sniff, chew, swallow or destroy. Many are obvious; others are not. Do a thorough advance house check to remove or rearrange those things that could hurt your puppy, keeping any potentially dangerous items out of areas to which he will have access.

Electrical cords are especially dangerous, since puppies view them as irresistible chew toys. Unplug and remove all exposed cords or fasten them beneath a baseboard where the puppy cannot reach them. Veterinarians and fire-fighters can tell you horror stories about electrical burns and house fires that resulted from dog-chewed electrical cords. Consider this a most serious precaution for your puppy and the rest of your family.

Scout your home for tiny objects that might be seen at a pup's eye level. Keep medication bottles and cleaning supplies well out of reach, and do the same with waste baskets and other trash containers. It goes without saying that you should not use rodent poison or other toxic chemicals in any area to which your dog has access and that you must keep such containers safely locked up. You will be amazed at how many places a curious puppy can discover!

KEEP OUT OF REACH

Most dogs don't browse around your medicine cabinet, but accidents do happen! The drug acetaminophen, the active ingredient in certain popular over-the-counter pain relievers, can be deadly to dogs and cats if ingested. Acetaminophen toxicity, caused by the dog's swallowing 15 to 20 tablets, can be manifested in abdominal pains within a day or two of ingestion, as well as liver damage. If you suspect your dog has swiped a bottle of pills, get the dog to the vet immediately so that the vet can induce vomiting and cleanse the dog's stomach.

A Dog-Safe Home

The dog-safety police are taking you on a house tour. Let's go room by room and see how safe your own home is for your new pup. The following items are doggie dangers, so either they must be removed or the dog should be monitored in or not have access to these areas.

Living Room
- house plants (some varieties are poisonous)
- fireplace or wood-burning stove
- paint on the walls (lead-based paint is toxic)
- lead drapery weights (toxic lead)
- lamps and electrical cords
- carpet cleaners or deodorizers

Outdoor
- swimming pool
- pesticides
- toxic plants
- lawn fertilizers

Bathroom
- blue water in the toilet bowl
- medicine cabinet (filled with potentially deadly bottles)
- soap bars, bleach, drain cleaners, etc.
- tampons

Kitchen
- household cleaners in the kitchen cabinets
- glass jars and canisters
- sharp objects (like kitchen knives, scissors and forks)
- garbage can (with remnants of good-smelling things like onions, potato skins, apple or pear cores, peach pits, coffee beans, etc.)
- food left out on counters (some "people foods" are toxic to dogs or will cause digestive upset)

Garage
- antifreeze
- fertilizers (including rose foods)
- pesticides and rodenticides
- pool supplies (chlorine and other chemicals)
- oil and gasoline in containers
- sharp objects, electrical cords and power tools

When your Beardie pup first arrives home, he will want to sniff out every new thing he comes across. This is how he gets acquainted with his new surroundings and his new family members.

Once your house has cleared inspection, check your yard. A sturdy fence, well embedded into the ground, will give your dog a safe place to play and potty. Bearded Collies are athletic, agile and bouncy dogs, so a 6-foot-high or higher fence is required to contain an agile youngster or adult. Check the fence periodically for necessary repairs. If there is a weak link or space to squeeze through, you can be sure a determined Bearded Collie will discover it.

The garage and shed can be hazardous places for a pup, as things like fertilizers, chemicals and tools are usually kept there. It's best to keep these areas off-limits to the dog. Antifreeze is especially dangerous to dogs, as they find the taste appealing and

it takes only a few licks from the driveway to kill a dog, puppy or adult.

VISITING THE VETERINARIAN
A good veterinarian is your Bearded Collie puppy's best health-insurance policy. If you do not already have a vet, ask your breeder, friends and experienced dog people in your area for recommendations so that you can select a vet who knows the breed, or at least herding breeds, before you bring your Bearded Collie puppy home. Also arrange for your puppy's first veterinary examination beforehand, since many vets do not have appointments immediately available and your puppy should visit the vet within a day or so of coming home.

It's important to make sure your puppy's first visit to the vet is a pleasant and positive one. The vet should take great care to befriend the pup and handle him

TOXIC PLANTS
Plants are natural puppy magnets, but many can be harmful, even fatal, if ingested by a puppy or adult dog. Scout your yard and home interior and remove any plants, bushes or flowers that could be even mildly dangerous. It could save your puppy's life. You can obtain a complete list of toxic plants from your veterinarian, at the public library or by looking online.

gently to make their first meeting a positive experience. The vet will give the pup a thorough physical examination and set up a schedule for vaccinations and other necessary wellness visits. Be sure to show your vet any health and inoculation records, which you should have received from your breeder. Your vet is a great source of canine health information, so be sure to ask questions and take notes. Creating a health journal for your puppy will make a handy reference for his wellness and any future health problems that may arise.

MEETING THE FAMILY

Your Bearded Collie's homecoming is an exciting time for all members of the family, and it's only natural that everyone will be eager to meet him, pet him and play with him. However, for the puppy's sake, it's best to make these initial family meetings as uneventful as possible so that the pup is not overwhelmed with too much too soon. Remember, he has just left his dam and his littermates and is away from the breeder's home for the first time. Despite his fuzzy wagging tail, he is still apprehensive and wondering where he is and who all these strange humans are. It's best to let him explore on his own and meet the family members as he feels comfortable. Let him investigate all the new smells,

ASK THE VET

Help your vet help you to become a well-informed dog owner. Don't be shy about becoming involved in your puppy's veterinary care by asking questions and gaining as much knowledge as you can. For starters, ask what shots your puppy is getting and what diseases they prevent, and discuss with your vet the safest way to vaccinate. Find out what is involved in your dog's annual wellness visits. If you plan to spay or neuter, discuss the best age at which to have this done. Start out on the right "paw" with your puppy's vet and develop good communication with him, as he will care for your dog's health throughout the dog's entire life.

sights and sounds at his own pace. Children should be especially careful to not get overly excited, use loud voices or hug the pup too tightly. Be calm, gentle and affectionate, and be ready to comfort him if he appears frightened or uneasy.

Be sure to show your puppy his new crate during this first day home. Toss a treat or two inside the crate; if he associates the crate with food, he will associate the crate with good things. If he is comfortable with the crate, you can offer him his first meal inside it. Leave the door ajar so he can wander in and out as he chooses.

FIRST NIGHT IN HIS NEW HOME

So much has happened in your Bearded Collie puppy's first day away from the breeder. He's had his first car ride to his new home. He's met his new human family and perhaps the other family pets. He has explored his new house and yard, at least those places where he is to be allowed during his first weeks at home. He may have visited his new veterinarian. He has eaten his first meal or two away from his dam and litter-mates. Surely that's enough to tire out an eight-week-old Bearded Collie pup...or so you hope!

It's bedtime. During the day, the pup investigated his crate, which is his new den and sleep-ing space, so it is not entirely strange to him. Line the crate with a soft towel or blanket that he can snuggle into and gently place him into the crate for the night. Some breeders send home a piece of bedding from where the pup slept with his littermates, and those familiar scents are a great comfort for the puppy on his first night without his siblings.

He will probably whine or cry. The puppy is objecting to the confinement and the fact that he is alone for the first time. This can be a stressful time for you as well as for the pup. It's important that you remain strong and don't let the puppy out of his crate to comfort him. He will fall asleep

eventually. If you release him, the puppy will learn that crying means "out" and will continue that habit. You are laying the groundwork for future habits. Some breeders find that soft music can soothe a crying pup and help him get to sleep.

SOCIALIZING YOUR PUPPY

The first 20 weeks of your Bearded Collie puppy's life are the most important of his entire lifetime. A properly socialized puppy will grow up to be a confi-dent and stable adult who will be a pleasure to live with and a well-mannered, welcome addition to the neighborhood.

The importance of socializa-tion cannot be overemphasized.

Research on canine behavior has proven that puppies who are not exposed to new sights, sounds, people and animals during their first 20 weeks of life will grow up to be timid and fearful, even aggressive, and unable to flourish outside of their familiar home environment.

Socializing your puppy is not difficult and, in fact, will be a fun breed, everyone will enjoy meeting "the new kid on the block." Take him for short walks to the park and to other dog-friendly places where he will encounter new people, especially children. Puppies automatically recognize children as "little people" and are drawn to play with them. Just make sure that you supervise these meetings and that the chil-

It is a good idea to supervise your Beardie's introduction to the family cat. Who says cats and dogs don't get along?

time for you both. Lead training goes hand in hand with socialization, so your puppy will be learning how to walk on a lead at the same time that he's meeting the neighborhood. Because the Bearded Collie is such a terrific dren do not get too rough or encourage him to play too hard. An overzealous pup can often nip too hard, frightening the child and in turn making the puppy overly excited. A bad experience in puppyhood can impact a dog for life, so a pup that has a negative experience with a child may grow up to be shy or even aggressive around children.

Take your puppy along on your daily errands. Puppies are natural "people magnets," and most people who see your pup will want to pet him. All of these encounters will help to mold him into a confident adult dog. Likewise, you will soon feel like a confident, responsible dog owner, rightly proud of your mannerly Bearded Collie.

Be especially careful of your puppy's encounters and experiences during the eight-to-ten-week-old period, which is also called the "fear period." This is a serious imprinting period, and all contact during this time should be gentle and positive. A frightening or negative event could leave a permanent impression that could affect his future behavior if a similar situation arises.

Also make sure that your puppy has received his first and second rounds of vaccinations before you expose him to other dogs or bring him to places that other dogs may frequent. Avoid dog parks and other strange-dog areas until your vet assures you that your puppy is fully immunized and resistant to the diseases that can be passed between canines. Discuss safe timing of socialization with your breeder and your vet.

LEADER OF THE PUPPY'S PACK
Like other canines, your puppy needs an authority figure, someone he can look up to and regard as the leader of his "pack." His first pack leader was his dam, who taught him to be polite and not chew too hard on her ears or nip at her muzzle. He learned those same lessons from his littermates. If he played too rough, they cried in pain and stopped the game, which sent an important message to the rowdy puppy.

As puppies play together, they are also struggling to determine who will be the boss. Being pack animals, dogs need someone to be in charge. If a litter of puppies remained together beyond puppyhood, one of the pups would emerge as the strongest one, the one who calls the shots.

Once your puppy leaves the pack, he will look intuitively for a new leader. If he does not recognize you as that leader, he will try to assume that position for himself. Of course, it is hard to

REPEAT YOURSELF
Puppies learn best through repetition. Use the same verbal cues and commands when teaching your puppy new behaviors or correcting for misbehaviors. Be consistent, but not monotonous. Puppies get bored just like puppy owners.

imagine your adorable Bearded Collie puppy trying to be in charge when he is so small and seemingly helpless. You must remember that these are natural canine instincts. Do not cave in and allow your pup to get the upper "paw"!

Just as socialization is so important during these first 20 weeks, so too is your puppy's early education. He was born without any bad habits. He does not know what is good or bad behavior. If he does things like nipping and digging, it's because he is having fun and doesn't know that humans consider these things as "bad." It's your job to

ESTABLISH A ROUTINE
Routine is very important to a puppy's learning environment. To facilitate house-training, use the same exit/entrance door for potty trips and always take the puppy to the same place in the yard. The same principle of consistency applies to all other aspects of puppy training.

teach him proper puppy manners, and this is the best time to accomplish that...before he has developed bad habits, since it is much more difficult to "unlearn" or correct unacceptable learned behavior than to teach good behavior from the start.

Make sure that all members of the family understand the importance of being consistent when training their new puppy. If you tell the puppy to stay off the sofa and your daughter allows him to cuddle on the couch with her to watch her favorite TV show, your pup will be confused about what he is and is not allowed to do. Have a family conference before your pup comes home so that every-one understands the basic princi-ples of puppy training and the rules you have set forth for the pup and agrees to follow them.

The old adage that "an ounce of prevention is worth a pound of cure" is especially true when it comes to puppies. It is much

A wire crate is a good choice for your Bearded Collie, as it is convenient for travel and affords the dog a full view of everything going on around him.

easier to prevent inappropriate behavior than it is to change it. It's also easier and less stressful for the pup, since it will keep discipline to a minimum and create a more positive learning environment for him. That, in turn, will also be easier on you!

SOLVING PUPPY PROBLEMS

CHEWING AND NIPPING

Nipping at fingers and toes is normal puppy behavior. Chewing is also the way that puppies investigate their surroundings. However, you will have to teach your puppy that chewing anything other than his toys is not acceptable. That won't

happen overnight, and at times puppy teeth will test your patience. However, if you allow nipping and chewing to continue, just think about the damage that a mature Bearded Collie can do with a full set of adult teeth.

Whenever your puppy nips your hand or fingers, cry out "Ouch!" in a loud voice, which should startle your puppy and stop him from nipping, even if only for a moment. Immediately distract him by offering a small treat or an appropriate toy for him to chew instead (which means having chew toys and puppy treats handy or in your pockets at all times). Praise him when he takes the toy and tell

Your puppy's early socialization began with his littermates. It is your responsibility to continue this process after you take your puppy home.

Exploring with a young friend, this Beardie pup is getting to know the "lay of the land" in his new back yard.

him what a good fellow he is. Praise is just as or even more important in puppy training as discipline and correction.

Puppies also tend to nip at children more often than adults, since they perceive little ones to be more vulnerable and more similar to their littermates. Further, some herding breeds nip at ankles and heels, extending their instincts to their human "flock." Teach your family members appropriate responses to nipping behavior. If children are unable to handle it themselves, you may have to intervene. Puppy nips can be quite painful, and a child's frightened reaction will only encourage a puppy to nip

harder, which is a natural canine response. As with all other puppy situations, interaction between your Bearded Collie puppy and children should be supervised.

Chewing on objects, not just family members' fingers and ankles, is also normal canine behavior that can be especially tedious (for the owner, not the pup) during the teething period when the puppy's adult teeth are coming in. At this stage, chewing just plain feels good. Furniture legs and cabinet corners are common puppy favorites. Shoes and other personal items also taste pretty good to a pup.

The best solution is, once again, prevention. If you value

something, keep it tucked away and out of reach. You can't hide your dining-room table in a closet, but you can try to deflect the chewing by applying a bitter product made just to deter dogs from chewing. Available in a spray or cream, this substance is vile-tasting, although safe for dogs, and most puppies will avoid the forbidden object after one tiny taste. You also can apply the product to your leather leash if the puppy tries to chew on his lead during leash-training sessions.

Keep a ready supply of safe chews handy to offer your Bearded Collie as a distraction when he starts to chew on something that's a "no-no." Remember, at this tender age he does not yet know what is permitted or forbidden, so you have to be "on call" every minute he's awake and on the prowl.

You may lose a treasure or two during puppy's growing-up period, and the furniture could sustain a nasty nick or two. These can be trying times, so be prepared for those inevitable accidents and comfort yourself in knowing that this too shall pass.

Puppy Whining
Puppies often cry and whine, just as infants and little children do. It's their way of telling us that they are lonely or in need of attention. Your puppy will miss his littermates and will feel insecure when he is left alone. You may be out of the house or just in another room, but he will still feel alone. During these times, the puppy's crate should be his personal comfort station, a place all his own where he can feel safe and secure. Once he learns that being alone is okay and not something to be feared, he will settle down without crying or objecting. You might want to leave a radio on while he is crated, as the sound of human voices can be soothing and will give the impression that people are around.

THE FAMILY FELINE
A resident cat has feline squatter's rights. The cat will treat the newcomer (your puppy) as she sees fit, regardless of what you do or say, so it's best to let the two of them work things out on their own terms. Cats have a height advantage and will generally leap to higher ground to avoid direct contact with a rambunctious pup. Some will hiss and boldly swat at a pup who passes by or tries to reach the cat. Keep the puppy under control in the presence of the cat and they will eventually become accustomed to each other.

Here's a hint: move the cat's litter box where the puppy can't get into it! It's best to do so well before the pup comes home so the cat is used to the new location.

Give your puppy a favorite cuddly toy or chew toy to entertain him whenever he is crated. You will both be happier: the puppy because he is safe in his den and you because he is quiet, safe and not getting into puppy escapades that can wreak havoc in your house or cause him danger.

To make sure that your puppy will always view his crate as a safe and cozy place, never, *ever*, use the crate as punishment. That's the best way to turn the crate into a negative place that the pup will want to avoid. Sure, you can use the crate for your own peace of mind if your puppy is getting into trouble and needs some "time out." Just don't let him know that! Never scold the pup and immediately place him into the crate. Count to ten, give him a couple of hugs and maybe a treat, then scoot him into his crate.

It's also important not to make a big fuss when he is released from the crate. That will make getting out of the crate more appealing than being in the crate, which is just the opposite of what you are trying to achieve.

"COUNTER SURFING"
What we like to call "counter surfing" is a normal extension of the dog's tendency to jump up, something at which Beardies excel, and usually starts to happen as soon as a puppy realizes that he is big enough to stand on his hind legs and investigate the good stuff on the kitchen counter or the coffee table. Once again, you have to be there to prevent it! As soon as you see your Bearded Collie even start to raise himself up, startle him with a sharp "No!" or "Aaahh, aaahh!" If he succeeds and manages to get one or both paws on the forbidden surface, remove his paws from the surface as you tell him "Off!" As soon as he's back on all four paws, command him to sit and praise him at once.

For surf prevention, make sure to keep any tempting treats or edibles out of reach, where your Bearded Collie can't see or smell them. It's the old rule of prevention yet again.

Your puppy's water intake should be carefully monitored during the housebreaking process. Remember—what goes in must come out and, with pups, it comes out rather quickly.

PROPER CARE OF YOUR

BEARDED COLLIE

Adding a Bearded Collie to your household means adding a new family member who will need your care each and every day. When your Bearded Collie pup first comes home, you will start a routine with him so that, as he grows up, your dog will have a daily schedule just as you do. The aspects of your dog's daily care will likewise become regular parts of your day, so you'll both have a new schedule. Dogs learn by consistency and thrive on routine; regular times for meals, exercise, grooming and potty trips are just as important for your dog as they are for you. Your dog's schedule will depend much on your family's daily routine, but remember that you now have a new member of the family who is part of your day every day.

FEEDING

Feeding your dog the best diet is based on various factors, including age, activity level, overall condition and size of breed. When you visit the breeder, he will share with you his advice about the proper diet for your dog based on his experience with the breed and the foods with which he has had success. Likewise, your vet will be a helpful source of advice throughout the dog's life and will aid you in planning a diet for optimal health.

FEEDING THE PUPPY

Of course, your pup's very first food will be his dam's milk. There may be special situations in which pups fail to nurse, necessitating that the breeder hand-feed them with a formula, but, for the most part, pups spend the first weeks of life nursing from their dam. The breeder weans the pups by gradually introducing solid foods and decreasing the milk meals. Pups may even start themselves off on the weaning process, albeit inadvertently, if they snatch bites from their mom's food bowl.

By the time the pups are ready for new homes, they are fully weaned and eating a good puppy food. As a new owner, you may be thinking, "Great! The breeder has taken care of the hard part." Not so fast. Puppies should initially be fed the same diet they received from the breeder, but if you choose to change the food, ask the breeder for advice.

A puppy's first year of life is the time when all or most of his growth and development takes place. This is a delicate time, and diet plays a huge role in proper skeletal and muscular formation. Improper diet and exercise habits can lead to damaging problems that will compromise the dog's health and movement for his entire life. That being said, new owners should not worry needlessly. With

Milk from their mother provides these Bearded Collie puppies with colostrum, which protects them during their first weeks of life.

DIET DON'TS

- Got milk? Don't give it to your dog! Dogs cannot tolerate large quantities of cows' milk, as they do not have the enzymes to digest lactose.
- You may have heard of dog owners who add raw eggs to their dogs' food for a shiny coat or to make the food more palatable, but consumption of raw eggs too often can cause a deficiency of the vitamin biotin.
- Avoid feeding table scraps, as they will upset the balance of the dog's complete food. Additionally, fatty or highly seasoned foods can cause upset canine stomachs.
- Do not offer raw meat to your dog. Raw meat can contain parasites; it also is high in fat.
- Vitamin A toxicity in dogs can be caused by too much raw liver, especially if the dog already gets enough vitamin A in his balanced diet, which should be the case.
- Bones like chicken, pork chop and other soft bones are not suitable, as they easily splinter.

the myriad types of food formulated specifically for growing pups of different-sized breeds, dog-food manufacturers have taken much of the guesswork out of feeding your puppy well. Since growth-food formulas are designed to provide the nutrition that a growing puppy needs, it is unnecessary and, in fact, can prove harmful to add supplements to the diet. Research has shown that too much of certain vitamin supplements and minerals predispose a dog to skeletal problems. It's by no means a case of "if a little is good, a lot is better." At every stage of your dog's life, too much or too little in the way of nutrients can be harmful, which is why a manufactured complete food is the easiest way to know that your dog is getting what he needs.

Because of a young pup's small body and accordingly small

Crunchy dry food and dog biscuits help keep a dog's teeth strong, clean and free from tartar.

Offer your young Beardie a puppy diet until he is about 12 months of age.

digestive system, his daily portion will be divided up into small meals throughout the day. This can mean starting off with three or more meals a day and decreasing the number of meals as the pup matures. For the adult, it is generally thought that dividing the day's food into two meals on a morning/evening schedule is healthiest for the dog's digestion.

Regarding the feeding schedule, feeding the pup at the same times and in the same place each day is important for both housebreaking purposes and establishing the dog's everyday routine. As for the amount to feed, growing puppies generally need proportionately more food per body weight than their adult counterparts, but a pup should never be allowed to gain excess weight. Dogs of all ages should be kept in proper body condition, but extra weight can strain a pup's developing frame, causing skeletal problems.

Watch your pup's weight as he grows and, if the recommended amounts seem to be too much or too little for your pup, consult the vet about appropriate dietary changes. Keep in mind that treats, although small, can quickly add up throughout the day, contributing unnecessary calories. Treats are fine when used prudently; opt for dog treats specially formulated to be healthy or for nutritious snacks like small pieces of cheese or cooked chicken.

FEEDING THE ADULT DOG

For the adult (meaning physically mature) dog, feeding properly is about maintenance, not growth. Again, correct weight is a concern. Your dog should appear fit and should have an evident "waist." His ribs should not be

protruding (a sign of being underweight), but they should be covered by only a slight layer of fat. Under normal circumstances, an adult dog can be maintained fairly easily with a high-quality nutritionally complete adult-formula food. I find that the majority of adult Beardies do not respond well to being fed on a high-protein diet. Therefore, if choosing an all-in-one food for an adult, choose the lower protein (pet) variety and not one for breeding or working animals.

Factor treats into your dog's overall daily caloric intake, and avoid offering table scraps. Not only are certain "people foods,"

NOT HUNGRY?

No dog in his right mind would turn down his dinner, would he? If you notice that your dog has lost interest in his food, there could be any number of causes. Dental problems are a common cause of appetite loss, one that is often overlooked. If your dog has a toothache, a loose tooth or sore gums from infection, chances are it doesn't feel so good to chew. Think about when you've had a toothache! If your dog does not approach the food bowl with his usual enthusiasm, look inside his mouth for signs of a problem. Whatever the cause, you'll want to consult your vet so that your chow hound can get back to his happy, hungry self as soon as possible.

like chocolate, onions, grapes, nuts and raisins, toxic to dogs but feeding from the table encourages begging and overeating. Over-weight dogs are more prone to health problems. Research has even shown that obesity takes years off a dog's life. With that in mind, resist the urge to overfeed and over-treat. Don't make unnec-essary additions to your dog's diet, whether with tidbits or with extra vitamins and minerals.

The amount of food needed for proper maintenance will vary depending on the individual dog's activity level, but you will be able to tell whether the daily portions are keeping him in good shape.

Consult your veterinarian for an acceptable maintenance diet for your adult Bearded Collie. Suggested portions are listed on the bag; you can modify them according to your dog's condition.

With the wide variety of good complete foods available, choosing what to feed is largely a matter of personal preference. Just as with the puppy, the adult dog should have consistency in his mealtimes and feeding place. In addition to a consistent routine, regular mealtimes also allow the owner to see how much his dog is eating. If the dog seems never to be satisfied or, likewise, becomes uninterested in his food, the owner will know right away that something is wrong and can consult the vet. Scheduled mealtimes also allow you to see that your Beardie has sufficient time to rest before and after mealtimes to promote digestive health and protect against a deadly but preventable condition called bloat, to which any breed can fall victim; discuss this with your breeder and vet.

SWITCHING FOODS

There are certain times in a dog's life when it becomes necessary to switch his food; for example, from puppy to adult food and then from adult to senior-dog food. Additionally, you may decide to feed your pup a different type of food from what he received from the breeder, and there may be "emergency" situations in which you can't find your dog's normal brand and have to offer something else temporarily. Anytime a change is made, for whatever reason, the switch must be done gradually. You don't want to upset the dog's stomach or end up with a picky eater who refuses to eat something new. A tried-and-true approach is, over the course of about a week, to mix a little of the new food in with the old, increasing the proportion of new to old as the days progress. At the end of the week, you'll be feeding his regular portions of the new food, and he will barely notice the change.

Diets for the Aging Dog

A good rule of thumb is that once a dog has reached 75% of his expected lifespan, he has reached "senior citizen" or geriatric status. Your Bearded Collie will be considered a senior at about 9 or 10 years of age; based on his size, he has a projected lifespan of about 12 to 14 years. Beardies tend to stay active into their double digits.

What does aging have to do with your dog's diet? No, he won't get a discount at the local diner's early-bird special. Yes, he will require some dietary changes to accommodate the changes that come along with increased age. One change is that the older dog's dietary needs become more similar to that of a puppy. Specifically, dogs can metabolize more protein as youngsters and seniors than in the adult-maintenance stage. Discuss with your vet whether you need to switch to a higher-

protein or senior-formulated food or whether your current adult-dog food contains sufficient nutrition for the senior.

Watching the dog's weight remains essential, even more so in the senior stage. Older dogs are already more vulnerable to illness, and obesity only contributes to their susceptibility to problems. As the older dog becomes less active and thus exercises less, his regular portions may cause him to gain weight. At this point, you may consider decreasing his daily food intake or switching to a reduced-calorie food. As with other changes, you should consult your vet for advice.

DON'T FORGET THE WATER!
For a dog, it's always time for a drink! Regardless of what type of food he eats, there's no doubt that he needs plenty of water. Fresh cold water, in a clean bowl, should be available to your dog. There are special circumstances, such as during puppy housebreaking, when you will want to monitor your pup's water intake so that you will be able to predict when he will need to relieve himself, but water must be available to him nonetheless. Water is essential for hydration and proper body function just as it is in humans.

You will get to know how much your dog typically drinks in a day. Of course, in the heat or if exercising vigorously, he will be

more thirsty and will drink more. However, if he begins to drink noticeably more water for no apparent reason, this could signal any of various problems, and you are advised to consult your vet.

Water is the best drink for dogs. Some owners are tempted to give milk from time to time or to moisten dry food with milk, but dogs do not have the enzymes necessary to digest the lactose in milk, which is much different from the milk that nursing puppies receive. Therefore, stick with clean, fresh water to quench your dog's thirst, and always have it readily available to him.

Whether at home or traveling, be sure to have water for your Bearded Collie.

EXERCISE

From my many years' experience, I feel that the absolute best and most natural exercise for Beardies is free running. This is a great deal more enjoyable for the dog than walking on a lead and usually much simpler for you. I think it is almost essential to have a large fenced yard and/or immediate access to another suitable enclosed area if you own a Beardie. Bearded Collies are dependent on plenty of exercise for their health and sanity, and for that of their owners! It's wonderful if you can participate in activities with your Beardie, bonding and exercising together. It goes

The Beardie is an exuberant dog who loves and needs exercise. This Bearded Collie is competing in an agility trial.

PUPPY STEPS

Puppies are brimming with activity and enthusiasm. It seems that they can play all day and night without tiring, but don't overdo your puppy's exercise regimen. Easy does it for the puppy's first six to nine months. Keep walks brief and don't let the puppy engage in stressful jumping games. The puppy frame is delicate, and too much exercise during those critical growing months can cause injury to his bone structure, ligaments and musculature. Save his first jog for his first birthday!

without saying that, although Beardies usually come when called, they should always run free in a safe area so they do not pose a nuisance or risk to themselves or others.

Puppies should be offered a level of free exercise appropriate to their age and development. Beardie puppies should be encouraged to take rest periods, as they will sometimes overtire themselves, especially when running with another dog. Exercising your adult dog with another dog is most enjoyable for the Beardie. Beardies generally get along well with other breeds, although their exuberance can sometimes overpower a small or timid dog.

Bear in mind that an overweight dog should never be

suddenly over-exercised; instead, he should be allowed to increase exercise slowly. Also remember that not only is exercise essential to keep the dog's body fit, it is essential to his mental well-being. A bored dog will find something to do, which often manifests itself in some type of destructive behavior. In this sense, exercise is just as essential for the owner's mental well-being!

GROOMING

As far as long-coated breeds go, I find that Beardies have one of the easier coats to care for. However, their coats do become abundant, so you should be very sure that you want to have this constant coat-care responsibility before you acquire a Beardie.

It is absolutely essential that you regularly groom your Beardie thoroughly from early puppy-

A COAT IN THE SUMMER

A dog's long or heavy coat is designed for insulation in any type of weather, so think again before giving your dog a summer haircut. Shaving down his coat in warm weather will affect his body's natural temperature regulation and is neither necessary nor beneficial.

hood. This not only keeps the coat growing in a healthy way but also ensures that your puppy knows that grooming is a part of his life. You can put the puppy on your lap or stand him on a table with a suitable non-slip surface. Use a fairly soft brush and groom the puppy all over. This is not a time for play, so don't let your puppy chew or play with the brush. Likewise, no growling or snapping is allowed. It is very important to show the puppy that this is seri-

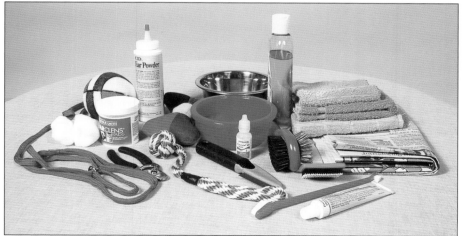

Your breeder can be a good source of advice regarding what grooming tools you will need for your Beardie. Purchase quality equipment that will withstand frequent use.

ous business, thus reinforcing that your puppy grows up knowing that there is no way out of being a well-groomed dog! At the same time, the experience should be a pleasurable one, so always give plenty of praise and end with pats and cuddles.

If you are having grooming problems, always consult an expert: the breeder of your dog, another Beardie exhibitor or an experienced owner. Usually one of these professionals will be happy to try to help you and your dog.

BATHING AND BRUSHING

Contrary to popular belief, you can regularly bathe your Beardie. Bathing will usually encourage the coat to maintain good condition, which in turn should make it easier to groom. Puppy coats respond well to bathing with puppy shampoos, but I always use a conditioner after shampooing. Remember to rinse the coat very thoroughly. As with brushing, bathing is serious business, and your puppy should be encouraged to see it in this light. Puppies will often be apprehensive of the bath and should have plenty of reas-

You can and should regularly bathe your Bearded Collie to keep the coat in good condition. Be sure to thoroughly brush the coat through before beginning the bath. Wet the coat down to the skin before applying shampoo; keep soap out of your Beardie's eyes and water away from his ears.

surance. The Beardie should be expected to stand politely in the bath and resist that strong Beardie urge to bounce and play!

After bathing, towel-dry and make sure that your puppy becomes fully dry in a warm atmosphere. Always brush the coat while it is still damp. In this way, the coat retains resistance to knot and tangle formation.

Puppies should also expect to have their ears and eyes looked at during bathing and drying so they are prepared for attention to these areas when they are adults. I find it best to continue to bathe the adult coat on a fairly regular basis. You should always use a shampoo and conditioning rinse formulated for dogs for best results.

As your Beardie's coat grows, it will alter in color and texture. A fluffy undercoat will combine with a harsher strong outer coat. Around six months or so, the first tangles and knots will start to appear, as if by magic. Behind the ears and between the legs will be prime targets, and the soft skin there makes it hard for a Beardie to accept the necessary grooming, at first. It is essential that you handle the dog appropriately at

After the bath, a blow dryer made for use on dogs is ideal for drying the coat, or you can use your own blow dryer on the lowest heat setting. During all grooming sessions, your Bearded Collie is expected to stand patiently for brushing, detangling and other routine tasks like ear cleaning.

Your Bearded Collie puppy should become accustomed to grooming at a young age or else it will be troublesome to groom him when he gets older.

sweeping strokes with the lie of the coat. I prefer to use a metal pin brush with blunted metal tips on a pneumatic rubber base. A metal slicker brush can also be useful for knot removal; it should be used totally flat and with some caution, as it may cause soreness to the skin if not used correctly. A wide-toothed metal comb is useful for ensuring that no small tangles remain at the end of a thorough grooming session.

I like to groom my dogs standing, but many people prefer them to lie down on one side and then the other. If you wish your

the stage of first removing knots. The dog must see that you are sympathetic but that you expect him to behave.

If you never intend to show your Beardie, you may decide to trim the hair behind the ears, on the tummy and between the front and hind legs. This can be done without outwardly spoiling the look of the coat at all. You may wish to have this done professionally, as there is a risk of cutting the delicate skin if not done with extreme care.

When grooming the longer Beardie coat, it is sensible to work systematically over the whole dog. Turn the coat so that the roots of the coat are exposed and brush from root to tip in long

dog to lie down for grooming, you will need to train him to accept being brushed this way from puppyhood, with love and reassurance.

MATS AND SPECIAL CONSIDERATIONS
Despite regular grooming, mats will sometimes occur. These should be removed by using an anti-tangle spray and gently teasing them out with the fingers and thumbs. Tease from the lower edge of the knot or mat towards the skin, pulling the knot apart and ensuring that you do not pull at the dog's skin. Brushing every so often as you tease the coat

A pin brush is effective in keeping the Beardie's coat tangle-free.

apart will help to open the knot. Special mat-breaking tools are available, which you might find useful. It is always necessary to completely comb through the coat after de-tangling and also to completely groom the dog after bathing. Any tangles left at this time will quickly escalate into difficult-to-manage mats in as short a time as a few days.

Most owners prefer to groom while the dog is standing or lying on a grooming table. The grooming table will make brushing your Beardie more comfortable for both of you.

If you have not tended to the dog's coat and he has developed a few matted areas, you should always groom the coat before bathing. The bathing process will "set" the mats and make their removal painful to the dog. Obviously, it is far better to groom regularly and thus prevent the bulkier tangles from forming.

You will need to gently pluck out the hair that grows inside your Beardie's ears. This is not painful to the dog if done properly.

The eyes of the Beardie require special attention. Ideally there should not be a lot of coat growth around the eyes of the adult Beardie, but the young dog may have fairly thick coat growth here. You can tie the coat up with a soft elastic hair band, but this should be removed if the Beardie is not being directly supervised, as he might remove the elastic and eat or choke on it.

Alternatively, you can trim above the eyes. This requires great care and is best done professionally if you are at all in doubt as to your abilities. Once the coat is trimmed, it will probably require regular re-trimming, as it will initially grow back thickly. However, if you leave the coat to mature naturally, it will grow and thin out with adulthood.

Beardie coats do change and undergo shedding. At these times, the undercoat has an increased tendency to mat into the top coat and frequent grooming is essential. Additionally, unspayed bitches will invariably lose a lot of coat around the time of and after their heat cycles. I find that my male Beardies tend to lose coat early in the year.

If you find that you really cannot cope with the dog's coat and you definitely know that you will never wish to show your dog, you can always resort to having the entire coat trimmed. This is a great pity, as you will no longer have the naturally beautiful longer coat, but it is certainly preferable to a matted, unhappy dog and a guilt-ridden owner. In fact, Beardies usually enjoy trimmed coats and feel free and airy, even much younger. Trimming the coat will mean that it is very hard to regain the full coat. Even though the Beardie's hair grows quickly, the full length will not be regained for two to three years, and then not without going through a hard-to-manage phase. Trimming should really be done professionally for best results. I would suggest that you ask for the dog to be trimmed and not clipped. Clipping the dog's coat will result in an ultra-short finish, which is, initially, rather unsightly and a bit of a shock to the dog in terms of comfort and draft-proofing!

EAR CLEANING

As your Beardie matures, the hair in his ears will grow and need attention. Using the thumb and forefinger, pluck the hair gently from the ears. The hair in this area is very soft and comes away fairly easily. If you use a very light sprinkling of a veterinary-approved ear powder, the process is easier. There is some brief discomfort to the dog but, since leaving the hair in the ears promotes canker formation, removing the hair is preferable. After clearing the ear of hair and leaving the skin to settle, use a soft wipe with a veterinary-approved ear cleanser to remove waxy deposits. Be on the lookout for any signs of infection or ear mite infestation. If your Bearded Collie has been shaking his head or scratching at his ears frequently, this usually indicates a problem. Any discharge or unpleasant smell should be checked by your veterinarian.

NAIL CLIPPING

Having his nails trimmed is not on many dogs' lists of favorite things to do. With this in mind, you will need to accustom your puppy to the procedure at a young age so that he will sit still (well,

as still as he can) for his pedicures. Long nails can cause the dog's feet to spread, which is not good for him; likewise, long nails can hurt if they unintentionally scratch, not good for you!

Some dogs' nails are worn down naturally by regular walking on hard surfaces, so the frequency with which you clip depends on your individual dog. Look at his

---

EYE CARE

During grooming sessions, pay extra attention to the condition of your dog's eyes. If the area around the eyes is soiled or if tear staining has occurred, there are various cleaning agents made especially for this purpose. Look at the dog's eyes to make sure no debris has entered; dogs with large eyes and those who spend time outdoors are especially prone to this. Use boiled water that has been cooled as an eye wash if needed.

The signs of an eye infection are obvious: mucus, redness, puffiness, scabs or other signs of irritation. If your dog's eyes become infected, the vet will likely prescribe an antibiotic ointment for treatment. If you notice signs of more serious problems, such as opacities in the eye, which usually indicate cataracts, consult the vet at once. Taking time to pay attention to your dog's eyes will alert you in the early stages of any problem so that you can get your dog treatment as soon as possible. You could save your dog's sight!

nails from time to time and clip as needed; a good way to know when it's time for a trim is if you hear your dog clicking as he walks across the floor.

There are several types of nail clippers and even electric nail-grinding tools made for dogs; first we'll discuss using the clipper. To start, have your clipper ready and some doggie treats on hand. You want your pup to view his nail-

SCOOTING HIS BOTTOM

Here's a doggy problem that many owners tend to neglect. If your dog is scooting his rear end around the carpet, he probably is experiencing anal-sac impaction or blockage. The anal sacs are the two grape-sized glands on either side of the dog's vent. The dog cannot empty these glands, which become filled with a foul-smelling material. The dog may attempt to lick the area to relieve the pressure. He may also rub his anus on your walls, furniture or floors.

Don't neglect your dog's rear end during grooming sessions. By squeezing both sides of the anus with a soft cloth, you can express some of the material in the sacs. If the material is pasty and thick, you likely will need the assistance of a veterinarian. Vets know how to express the glands and can show you how to do it correctly without hurting the dog or spraying yourself with the unpleasant liquid.

clipping sessions in a positive light, and what better way to convince him than with food? You may want to enlist the help of an assistant to comfort the pup and offer treats as you concentrate on the clipping itself. The guillotine-type clipper is thought of by many as the easiest type to use; the nail tip is inserted into the opening, and blades on the top and bottom snip it off in one clip.

Start by grasping the pup's paw; a little pressure on the foot pad causes the nail to extend, making it easier to clip. Clip off a little at a time. If you can see the "quick," which is a blood vessel that runs through each nail, you will know how much to trim, as you do not want to cut into the quick. On that note, if you do cut the quick, which will cause bleeding, you can stem the flow of blood with a styptic pencil or other clotting agent. If you mistakenly nip the quick, do not panic or fuss, as this will cause the pup to be afraid. Simply reassure the pup, stop the bleeding and move on to the next nail. Don't be discouraged; you will become a professional canine pedicurist with practice.

You may or may not be able to see the quick, so it's best to just clip off a small bit at a time. If you see a dark dot in the center of the nail, this is the quick and your cue to stop clipping. Tell the puppy he's a "good boy" and offer a piece of treat with each nail. You can also use nail-clipping time to examine the footpads, making sure that they are not dry and cracked and that nothing has become embedded in them.

The nail grinder, the other choice, is many owners' first choice. Accustoming the puppy to the sound of the grinder and sensation of the buzz presents fewer challenges than the clipper, and there's no chance of cutting through the quick. Use the grinder on a low setting and always talk soothingly to your dog. He won't mind his salon visit, and he'll have nicely polished nails as well; just make sure that no coat gets caught in the grinder.

IDENTIFICATION AND TRAVEL

ID FOR YOUR DOG

You love your Bearded Collie and want to keep him safe. Of course, you take every precaution to prevent his escaping from the yard or becoming lost or stolen. You have a sturdy high fence and you always keep your dog on lead when out and about in public places. If your dog is not properly identified, however, you are overlooking a major aspect of his safety. We hope to never be in a situation where our dog is missing, but we should practice prevention in the unfortunate case that this happens; identification greatly increases

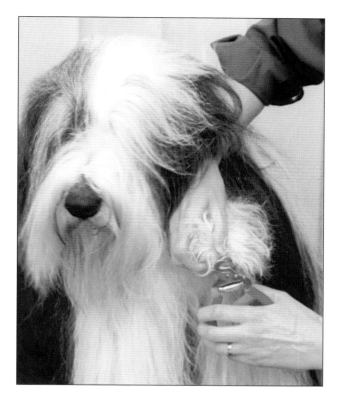

the chances of your dog's being returned to you.

There are several ways to identify your dog. First, the traditional dog tag should be a staple in your dog's wardrobe, attached to his everyday collar. Tags can be made of sturdy plastic and various metals and should include your contact information so that a person who finds the dog can get in touch with you right away to arrange his return. Many people today enjoy the wide range of decorative tags available, so have fun and create a tag to match your

When you cut your Beardie's nails, hold his foot steady with one hand and take off the end of each nail in one quick clip, using a nail clipper made for dogs.

microchips, and not all are compatible with the others' scanning devices. It's best to find a company with a universal microchip that can be read by scanners made by other companies as well. It won't do any good to have the dog chipped if the information cannot be retrieved. Also, not every humane society, shelter and clinic is equipped with a scanner, although more and more facilities are equipping themselves. In fact, many shelters microchip dogs that they adopt out to new homes.

Because the microchip is not visible to the eye, the dog must wear a tag that states that he is microchipped so that whoever picks him up will know to have him scanned. He of course also should have a tag with contact information in case his chip cannot be read. Humane societies and veterinary clinics offer microchipping service, which is usually very affordable.

Though less popular than microchipping, tattooing is another permanent method of ID for dogs. Most vets perform this service, and there are also clinics that perform dog tattooing. This is also an affordable procedure and one that will not cause much discomfort for the dog. It is best to put the tattoo in a visible area, such as the ear, to deter theft. It is sad to say that there are cases of dogs' being stolen and sold to

dog's personality. Of course, it is important that the tag stays on the collar, so have a secure "O" ring attachment; you also can explore the type of tag that slides right onto the collar.

In addition to the ID tag, which every dog should wear even if identified by another method, two other forms of identification have become popular: microchipping and tattooing. In microchipping, a tiny scannable chip is painlessly inserted under the dog's skin. The number is registered to you so that, if your lost dog turns up at a clinic or shelter, the chip can be scanned to retrieve your contact information.

The advantage of the microchip is that it is a permanent form of ID, but there are some factors to consider. Several different companies make research laboratories, but such laboratories will not accept tattooed dogs.

To ensure that the tattoo is effective in aiding your dog's return to you, the tattoo number must be registered with a national organization. That way, when someone finds a tattooed dog, a phone call to the registry will quickly match the dog with his owner.

HIT THE ROAD

Car travel with your Bearded Collie may be limited to necessity only, such as trips to the vet, or you may bring your dog along almost everywhere you go. This will depend much on your individual dog and how he reacts to rides in the car. You can begin desensitizing your dog to car travel as a pup so that it's something that he's used to. Still, some dogs suffer from motion sickness. Your vet may prescribe a medication for this if trips in the car pose a problem for your dog. At the very least, you will need to get him to the vet, so he will need to tolerate these trips with the least amount of hassle possible.

The safest way for your Beardie to travel is in a crate. Driving with a dog loose in a car can be very dangerous to both the dog and the driver.

uses in the home. Other options include a car harness (like a seat belt for dogs) and partitioning the back of the car with a gate made for this purpose.

Bring along what you will need for the dog. He should wear his collar and ID tags, of course, and you should bring his leash, water (and food if a long trip) and clean-up materials for potty breaks and in case of motion sickness. Always keep your dog on his leash when you make stops, and never leave him alone in the car. Many a dog has died from the heat inside a closed car; this does not take much time at all in any kind of weather. A dog left alone inside a car can also be a target for thieves.

Start taking your pup on short trips, maybe just around the block to start. If he is fine with short trips, lengthen your rides a little at a time. Start to take him on your errands or just for drives around town. By this time, it will be easy to tell whether your dog is a born traveler or would prefer staying at home when you are on the road.

Of course, safety is a concern for dogs in the car. First, he must travel securely, not left loose to roam about the car where he could be injured or distract the driver. A young pup can be held by a passenger initially but should soon graduate to a travel crate, which can be the same crate he

DOGGONE!

Wendy Ballard is the editor and publisher of the *DogGone*™ newsletter, which comes out bi-monthly and features fun articles by dog owners who love to travel with their dogs. The newsletter includes information about fun places to go with your dogs, including popular vacation spots, dog-friendly hotels, parks, campgrounds, resorts, etc., as well as interesting activities to do with your dog, such as flyball, agility and much more. You can subscribe to the publication by contacting the publisher at PO Box 651155, Vero Beach, FL 32965-1155.

BOARDING

Today there are many options for dog owners who need someone to care for their dogs in certain circumstances. While many think of boarding their dogs as something to do when away on vacation, many others use the services of doggie "daycare" facilities, dropping their dogs off to spend the day while they are at work. Many of these facilities offer both long-term and daily care. Many go beyond just boarding and cater to all sorts of needs, with on-site grooming, veterinary care, training classes and even "web-cams" where owners can log onto the internet and check out what their dogs are up to. Most dogs enjoy the activity and time spent with other dogs.

Before you need to use such a service, check out the ones in your area. Make visits to see the facilities, meet the staff, discuss fees and available services and see whether this is a place where you

think your dog will be happy. It is best to do your research in advance so that you're not stuck at the last minute, forced into making a rushed decision without knowing whether the kennel that you've chosen meets your standards. You also can check with your vet's office to see whether they offer boarding for their clients or can recommend a good kennel in the area.

The kennel will need to see proof of your dog's health records and vaccinations so as not to spread illness from dog to dog. Your dog also will need proper identification. Owners usually experience some separation anxiety the first time they have to leave their dog in someone else's care, so it's reassuring to know that the kennel you choose is run by experienced, caring, true dog people.

Visit some local boarding facilities in advance of your trip so that you can make a choice ahead of time and know that you will be comfortable with where your dog is staying.

Your Beardie will enjoy exploring new places when you travel, but never let him roam free and always make sure he is properly identified.

BEARDED COLLIE

BASIC TRAINING PRINCIPLES: PUPPY VS. ADULT

There's a big difference between training an adult dog and training a young puppy. With a young puppy, everything is new. At eight to ten weeks of age, he will be experiencing many things, and he has nothing with which to compare these experiences. Up to this point, he has been with his dam and littermates, not one-on-one with people except in his interactions with his breeder and visitors to the litter.

When you first bring the puppy home, he is eager to please you. This means that he accepts doing things your way. During the next couple of months, he will absorb the basis of everything he needs to know for the rest of his life. This early age is even referred to as the "sponge" stage. After that, for the next 18 months, it's up to you to reinforce good manners by building on the foundation that you've established. Once your puppy is reliable in basic commands and behavior and has reached the appropriate age, you may gradually introduce him to some of the interesting sports, games and activities available to pet owners and their dogs.

Raising your puppy is a family affair. Each member of the family must know what rules to set forth for the puppy and how to use the same one-word commands to mean exactly the same thing every time. Even if yours is a large family, one person will soon be considered by the pup to be the leader, the Alpha person in his pack, the "boss" who must be obeyed. Often that highly regarded person turns out to be the one who feeds the puppy. Food ranks very high on the puppy's list of important things!

KNOW THE BASICS

1. Start training early. A young puppy is ready, willing and able.
2. Timing is your all-important tool. Praise at the exact time that the dog responds correctly. Pay close attention.
3. Patience is almost as important as timing!
4. Repeat! The same word has to mean the same thing every time.
5. In the beginning, praise all correct behavior verbally, along with treats and petting.

BE UPSTANDING!
You are the dog's leader. During training, stand up straight so your dog looks up at you, and therefore up *to* you. Say the command words distinctly, in a clear, declarative tone of voice. (No barking!) Give rewards only as the correct response takes place (remember your timing!). Praise, smiles and treats are "rewards" used to positively reinforce correct responses. Don't repeat a mistake. Just change to another exercise—you will soon find success!

That's why your puppy is rewarded with small treats along with verbal praise when he responds to you correctly. As the puppy learns to do what you want him to do, the food rewards are gradually eliminated and only the praise remains. If you were to keep up with the food treats, you could have two problems on your hands—an obese dog and a beggar.

Training begins the minute your Bearded Collie puppy steps through the doorway of your home, so don't make the mistake of putting the puppy on the floor and telling him by your actions to "Go for it! Run wild!" Even if this is your first puppy, you must act as if you know what you're doing: be the boss. An uncertain pup may be terrified to move, while a bold one will be ready to take you

at your word and start plotting to destroy the house! Before you collected your puppy, you decided where his own special place would be, and that's where to put him when you first arrive home. Give him a house tour after he has investigated his area and had a nap and a bathroom "pit stop."

It's worth mentioning here that, if you've adopted an adult dog that is completely trained to your liking, lucky you! You're off the hook! However, if that dog spent his life up to this point in a kennel, or even in a good home but without any real training, be prepared to tackle the job ahead. A dog three years of age or older with no previous training cannot be blamed for not knowing what he was never taught. While the dog is trying to understand and learn your rules, at the same time he has to unlearn many of his previously self-taught habits and general view of the world.

Working with a professional trainer will speed up your progress with an adopted adult dog. You'll need patience, too. Some new rules may be close to impossible for the dog to accept. After all, he's been successful so far by doing everything his way! (Patience again.) He may agree with your instruction for a few days and then slip back into his old ways, so you must be just as consistent and understanding in your teaching as you would be with a puppy. (More patience needed yet again!) Your dog has to learn to pay attention to your voice, your family, the daily routine, new smells, new sounds and, in some cases, even a new climate.

One of the most important things to find out about a newly adopted adult dog is his reaction to children (yours and others), strangers and your friends, and how he acts upon meeting other dogs. If he was not socialized with dogs as a puppy, this could be a major problem. This does not mean that he's a "bad" dog, a vicious dog or an aggressive dog; rather, it means that he has no idea how to read another dog's body language. There's no way for him to tell whether the other dog is a friend or foe. Survival instinct takes over, telling him to attack first and ask questions later. This definitely calls for professional help and, even then, may not be a behavior that can be corrected 100% reliably (or even at all). If you have a puppy, this is why it is so very important to introduce your young puppy properly to other puppies and "dog-friendly" adult dogs.

HOUSE-TRAINING YOUR BEARDED COLLIE
Dogs are tactility-oriented when it comes to house-training. In other words, they respond to the surface on which they are given approval

Consistency is the key to housebreaking your Bearded Collie. Take him to the same place to relieve himself each time and it will become a habit for him.

to eliminate. The choice is yours (the dog's version is in parentheses): The lawn (including the neighbors' lawns)? A bare patch of earth under a tree (where people like to sit and relax in the summertime)? Concrete steps or patio (all sidewalks, garages and basement floors)? The curbside (watch out for cars)? A small area of crushed stone in a corner of the yard (mine!)? The latter is the best

choice if you can manage it, because it will remain strictly for the dog's use and is easy to keep clean.

You can start out with paper-training indoors and switch over to an outdoor surface as the puppy matures and gains control over his need to eliminate. For the nay-sayers, don't worry—this won't mean that the dog will soil on every piece of newspaper

lying around the house. You are training him to go outside, remember? Starting out by paper-training often is the only choice for a city dog.

WHEN YOUR PUPPY'S "GOT TO GO"
Your puppy's need to relieve himself is seemingly non-stop, but signs of improvement will be seen each week. From 8 to 10 weeks old, the puppy will have to be taken outside every time he wakes up, about 10–15 minutes after every meal and after every period of play—all day long, from first thing in the morning until his bedtime! That's a total of ten or more trips per day to teach the puppy where it's okay to relieve himself. With that schedule in mind, you can see that house-training a young puppy is not a part-time job. It requires someone to be home all day.

If that seems overwhelming or impossible, do a little planning. For example, plan to pick up your puppy at the start of a vacation period. If you can't get home in the middle of the day, plan to hire a dog-sitter or ask a neighbor to come over to take the pup outside, feed him his lunch and then take him out again about ten or so minutes after he's eaten. Also make arrangements with that or another person to be your "emergency" contact if you have to stay late on the job. Remind yourself—repeatedly—that this hectic schedule improves as the puppy gets older.

HOME WITHIN A HOME

Your Bearded Collie puppy needs to be confined to one secure, puppy-proof area when no one is able to watch his every move. Generally, the kitchen is the place of choice because the floor is washable. Likewise, it's a busy family area that will accustom the pup to a variety of noises, everything from pots and pans to the telephone, blender and dishwasher. He will also be enchanted by the smell of your cooking (and will never be critical when you burn something). An exercise pen (also called an "ex-pen," a puppy version of a playpen) within the room of choice is an excellent means of confinement for a young pup. He can see out and has a certain amount of space in which to run about, but he is safe from dangerous things like electrical cords, heating units, trash baskets or open kitchen-supply cabinets. Place the pen where the puppy will not get a blast of heat or air conditioning.

In the pen, you can put a few toys, his bed (which can be his crate if the dimensions of pen and crate are compatible) and a few layers of newspaper in one small corner, just in case. A water bowl can be hung at a convenient height on the side of the ex-pen so it won't become a splashing pool for an innovative puppy. His food dish can go on the floor, near but not under the water bowl.

Crates are something that pet owners are at last getting used to for their dogs. Wild or domestic canines have always preferred to sleep in den-like safe spots, and that is exactly what the crate provides. How often have you seen adult dogs that choose to sleep under a table or chair even though they have full run of the house? It's the den connection.

In your "happy" voice, use the word "Crate" every time you put the pup into his den. If he's new to a crate, toss in a small biscuit for him to chase the first few

---

DAILY SCHEDULE

How many relief trips does your puppy need per day? A puppy up to the age of 14 weeks will need to go outside about 8 to 12 times per day! You will have to take the pup out any time he starts sniffing around the floor or turning in small circles, as well as after naps, meals, games and lessons or whenever he's released from his crate. Once the puppy is 14 to 22 weeks of age, he will require only 6 to 8 relief trips. At the ages of 22 to 32 weeks, the puppy will require about 5 to 7 trips. Adult dogs typically require 4 relief trips per day, in the morning, afternoon, evening and late at night.

Canine Development Schedule

It is important to understand how and at what age a puppy develops into adulthood. If you are a puppy owner, consult the following Canine Development Schedule to determine the stage of development your puppy is currently experiencing. This knowledge will help you as you work with the puppy in the weeks and months ahead.

Period	Age	Characteristics
First to Third	Birth to Seven Weeks	Puppy needs food, sleep and warmth and responds to simple and gentle touching. Needs mother for security and disciplining. Needs littermates for learning and interacting with other dogs. Pup learns to function within a pack and learns pack order of dominance. Begin socializing pup with adults and children for short periods. Pup begins to become aware of his environment.
Fourth	Eight to Twelve Weeks	Brain is fully developed. Pup needs socializing with outside world. Remove from mother and littermates. Needs to change from canine pack to human pack. Human dominance necessary. Fear period occurs between 8 and 12 weeks. Avoid fright and pain.
Fifth	Thirteen to Sixteen Weeks	Training and formal obedience should begin. Less association with other dogs, more with people, places, situations. Period will pass easily if you remember this is pup's change-to-adolescence time. Be firm and fair. Flight instinct prominent. Permissiveness and over-disciplining can do permanent damage. Praise for good behavior.
Juvenile	Four to Eight Months	Another fear period about 7 to 8 months of age. It passes quickly, but be cautious of fright and pain. Sexual maturity reached. Dominant traits established. Dog should understand sit, down, come and stay by now.

Note: These are approximate time frames. Allow for individual differences in puppies.

The clock could drive the puppy nuts, and the hot-water bottle could end up as a very soggy waterbed! An extremely good breeder would have introduced your puppy to the crate by letting two pups sleep together for a couple of nights, followed by several nights alone. How thankful you will be if you found that breeder!

Safe toys in the pup's crate or area will keep him occupied, but monitor their condition closely. Discard any toys that show signs of being chewed to bits. Squeaky parts, bits of stuffing or plastic or any other small pieces can cause intestinal blockage or possibly choking if swallowed.

If you have a fenced yard, you can let the puppy go to his relief area on his own after he's used it a few times. Supervise him as he follows his nose to the spot.

times. At night, after he's been outside, he should sleep in his crate. The crate may be kept in his designated area at night or, if you want to be sure to hear those wake-up yips in the morning, put the crate in a corner of your bedroom. However, don't make any response whatsoever to whining or crying. If he's completely ignored, he'll settle down and get to sleep.

Good bedding for a young puppy is an old folded bath towel or an old blanket, something that is easily washable and disposable if necessary ("accidents" will happen!). Never put newspaper in the puppy's crate. Also, those old ideas about adding a clock to replace his mother's heartbeat, or a hot-water bottle to replace her warmth, are just that—old ideas.

TIDY BOY

Clean by nature, dogs do not like to soil their dens, which in effect are their crates or sleeping quarters. Unless not feeling well, dogs will not defecate or urinate in their crates. Crate training capitalizes on the dog's natural desire to keep his den clean. Be conscientious about giving the puppy as many opportunities to relieve himself outdoors as possible. Reward the puppy for correct behavior. Praise him and pat him whenever he "goes" in the correct location. Even the tidiest of puppies can have potty accidents, so be patient and dedicate more energy to helping your puppy achieve a clean lifestyle.

PROGRESSING WITH POTTY-TRAINING

After you've taken your puppy out and he has relieved himself in the area you've selected, he can have some free time with the family as long as there is someone responsible for watching him. That doesn't mean just someone in the same room who is watching TV or busy on the computer, but one person who is doing nothing other than keeping an eye on the pup, playing with him on the floor and helping him understand his position in the pack.

This first taste of freedom will let you begin to set the house rules. If you don't want the dog on the furniture, now is the time to prevent his first attempts to jump up onto the couch. The word to use in this case is "Off," not "Down." "Down" is the word you will use to teach the down position, which is something entirely different.

Most corrections at this stage come in the form of simply distracting the puppy. Instead of telling him "No" for "Don't chew the carpet," distract the chomping puppy with a toy and he'll forget about the carpet.

As you are playing with the pup, do not forget to watch him closely and pay attention to his body language. Whenever you see him begin to circle or sniff, take the puppy outside to relieve himself. If you are paper-training, put him back into his confined

EXTRA! EXTRA!

The headlines read: "Puppy Piddles Here!" Breeders commonly use newspapers to line their whelping pens, so puppies learn to associate newspapers with relieving themselves. Do not use newspapers to line your pup's crate, as this will signal to your puppy that it is OK to urinate in his crate. If you choose to paper-train your puppy, you will layer newspapers on a section of the floor near the door he uses to go outside. You should encourage the puppy to use the papers to relieve himself, and bring him there whenever you see him getting ready to go. Little by little, you will reduce the size of the newspaper-covered area so that the puppy will learn to relieve himself "on the other side of the door."

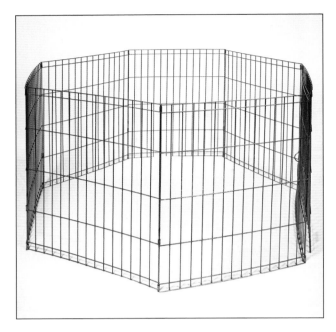

A wire ex-pen can be used, alone or in conjunction with the crate, to confine a pup. Make sure the sides are high enough to contain a bouncy Beardie, who may try to climb or jump out of the enclosure.

attraction is why it's so important to clean up any messes made in the house by using a product specially made to eliminate the odor of dog urine and droppings. Regular household cleansers won't do the trick. Pet shops sell the best pet deodorizers. Invest in the largest container you can find!

Scent attraction eventually will lead your pup to his chosen area on the newspapers. In either case, praise him as he eliminates while he actually is in the act of relieving himself. Three seconds after he has finished is too late! You'll be praising him for running toward you, or picking up a toy or whatever he may be doing at that moment, and that's not what you want to be praising him for. Timing is a vital tool in all dog training. Use it.

Remove soiled newspapers immediately and replace them with clean ones. You may want to take a small piece of soiled paper and place it in the middle of the new clean papers, as the scent will attract him to that spot when it's time to go again. That scent

SOMEBODY TO BLAME

House-training a puppy can be frustrating for the puppy and the owner alike. The puppy does not instinctively understand the difference between defecating on the pavement outside and on the ceramic tile in the kitchen. He is confused and frightened by his human's exuberant reactions to his natural urges. The owner, arguably the more intelligent of the duo, is also frustrated that he cannot convince his puppy to obey his commands and instructions.

In frustration, the owner may struggle with the temptation to discipline the puppy, scold him or even strike him on the rear end. These types of harsh correction are unnecessary and inappropriate, and will defeat your purpose in gaining your puppy's trust and respect. Don't blame your nine-week-old puppy. Blame yourself for not being 100% consistent in the puppy's lessons and routine. The lesson here is simple: try harder and your puppy will succeed.

spot outdoors; this is the basis of outdoor training. When you take your puppy outside to relieve himself, use a one-word command such as "Outside" or "Go-potty" (that's one word to the puppy!) as you pick him up and attach his leash. Then put him down in his area. If for any reason you can't carry him, snap the leash on quickly and lead him to his spot. Now comes the hard part—hard for you, that is. Just stand there until he urinates and defecates. Move him a few feet in one direction or another if he's just sitting there looking at you, but remember that this is neither playtime nor time for a walk. This is strictly a business trip! Then, as he circles and squats (remember your timing!), give him a quiet "Good dog" as praise. If you start to jump for joy, ecstatic over his performance, he'll do one of two things: either he will stop mid-stream, as it were, or he'll do it again for you—in the house—and expect you to be just as delighted!

Give him five minutes or so and, if he doesn't go in that time, take him back indoors to his confined area and try again in another ten minutes, or immediately if you see him sniffing and circling. By careful observation, you'll soon work out a successful schedule.

Accidents, by the way, are just that—accidents. Clean them up

POTTY COMMAND

Most dogs love to please their masters; there are no bounds to what dogs will do to make their owners happy. The potty command is a good example of this theory. If toileting on command makes the master happy, then more power to him. Puppies will obligingly piddle if it really makes their keepers smile. Some owners can be creative about which word they will use to command their dogs to relieve themselves. Some popular choices are "Potty," "Tinkle," "Piddle," "Let's go," "Hurry up" and "Toilet." Give the command every time your puppy goes into position and the puppy will begin to associate his business with the command.

quickly and thoroughly, without comment, after the puppy has been taken outside to finish his business and then put back into his area or crate. If you witness an accident in progress, say "No!" in a stern voice and get the pup outdoors immediately. No punishment is needed. You and your puppy are just learning each other's language, and sometimes it's easy to miss a puppy's message. Chalk it up to experience and watch more closely from now on.

TIPS FOR TRAINING AND SAFETY

1. Whether on- or off-leash, practice only in a fenced area.
2. Remove the training collar when the training session is over.
3. Don't try to break up a dogfight.
4. "Come," "Leave it" and "Wait" are safety commands.
5. The dog belongs in a crate or behind a barrier when riding in the car.
6. Don't ignore the dog's first sign of aggression. Aggression only gets worse, so take it seriously.
7. Keep the faces of children and dogs separated.
8. Pay attention to what the dog is chewing.
9. Keep the vet's number near your phone.
10. "Okay" is a useful release command.

KEEPING THE PACK ORDERLY

Discipline is a form of training that brings order to life. For example, military discipline is what allows the soldiers in an army to work as one. Discipline is a form of teaching and, in dogs, is the basis of how the successful pack operates. Each member knows his place in the pack and all respect the leader, or Alpha dog. It is essential for your puppy that you establish this type of relationship, with you as the Alpha, or leader. It is a form of social coexistence that all canines recognize and accept. Discipline, therefore, is never to be confused with punishment. When you teach your puppy how you want him to behave, and he behaves properly and you praise him for it, you are disciplining him with a form of positive reinforcement.

For a dog, rewards come in the form of praise, a smile, a cheerful tone of voice, a few friendly pats or a rub of the ears. Rewards are also small food treats. Obviously, that does not mean bits of regular dog food. Instead, treats are very small bits of special things like cheese or pieces of soft dog treats. The idea is to reward the dog with something very small that he can taste and swallow, providing instant positive reinforcement. If he has to take time to chew the treat, he will have forgotten what he did to earn it by the time he is finished!

Your puppy should never be physically punished. The displeasure shown on your face and in your voice is sufficient to signal to the pup that he has done something wrong. He wants to please everyone higher up on the social ladder, especially his leader, so a scowl and harsh voice will take care of the error. Growling out the word "Shame!" when the pup is caught in the act of doing something wrong is better than the repetitive "No." Some dogs hear "No" so often that they begin to think it's their name! By the way, do not use the dog's name when you're correcting him. His name is reserved to get his attention for something pleasant about to take place.

There are punishments that have nothing to do with you. For example, your dog may think that chasing cats is one reason for his existence. You can try to stop it as much as you like but without success, because it's such fun for the dog. But one good hissing, spitting swipe of a cat's claws

across the dog's nose will put an end to the game forever. Intervene only when your dog's eyeball is seriously at risk. Cat scratches can cause permanent damage to an innocent but annoying puppy.

PUPPY KINDERGARTEN

COLLAR AND LEASH

Before you begin your Bearded Collie puppy's education, he must be used to his collar and leash. Choose a collar for your puppy that is secure, but not heavy or bulky. He won't enjoy training if he's uncomfortable. A flat buckle collar is fine for everyday wear and for initial puppy training. For older dogs, there are several types of training collars such as the martingale, which is a double loop that tightens slightly around the neck, or the head collar,

Accustom your pup to his collar before you initiate the first lesson. For a puppy, his everyday buckle collar is the only collar you need for training.

"SCHOOL" MODE

When is your puppy ready for a lesson? Maybe not always when you are. Attempting training with treats just before his mealtime is asking for disaster. Notice what times of day he performs best and make that Fido's school time.

him to roam away from his area. The shorter leash will also be the one to use initially when you walk the puppy.

If you've been wise enough to enroll in a puppy kindergarten training class, suggestions will be made as to the best collar and leash for your young puppy. I say "wise" because your puppy will be in a class with puppies in his age range (up to five months old) of all breeds and sizes. It's the perfect way for him to learn the right way (and the wrong way) to interact with other dogs as well as

The time you invest in accustoming your Beardie to a leash will pay off when you have a well-behaved dog, walking nicely beside you rather than taking you for a walk.

which is similar to a horse's halter. Do not use a chain choke collar with your Beardie, as it will pull and damage the long coat. Ask your breeder about suitable training collars for the breed.

A lightweight 6-foot woven cotton or nylon training leash is preferred by most trainers because it is easy to fold up in your hand and comfortable to hold because there is a certain amount of give to it. There are lessons where the dog will start off 6 feet away from you at the end of the leash. The leash used to take the puppy outside to relieve himself is shorter because you don't want

DON'T STRESS ME OUT
Your dog doesn't have to deal with paying the bills, the daily commute, PTA meetings and the like, but, believe it or not, there's a lot of stress in a dog's world. Stress can be caused by the owner's impatient demeanor and his angry or harsh corrections. If your dog cringes when you reach for his training collar, he's stressed. An older dog is sometimes stressed out when he goes to a new home. No matter what the cause, put off all training until he's over it. If he's going through a fear period—shying away from people, trembling when spoken to, avoiding eye contact or hiding under furniture—wait to resume training. Naturally you'd also postpone your lessons if the dog were sick, and the same goes for you. Show some compassion.

When trying to keep the pup focused on the lesson, there's nothing like a tasty tidbit to convince him to pay attention.

their people. You cannot teach your puppy how to interpret another dog's sign language. For a first-time puppy owner, these socialization classes are invaluable. For experienced dog owners, they are a real boon to further training.

ATTENTION
You've been using the dog's name since the minute you collected him from the breeder, so you should be able to get his attention by saying his name—with a big smile and in an excited tone of voice. His response will be the puppy equivalent of "Here I am! What are we going to do?" Your immediate response (if you haven't guessed by now) is "Good dog." Rewarding him at the moment he pays attention to you teaches him the proper way to respond when he hears his name.

EXERCISES FOR A BASIC CANINE EDUCATION

THE SIT EXERCISE
There are several ways to teach the puppy to sit. The first one is

---

WHO'S TRAINING WHOM?

Dog training is a black-and-white exercise. The correct response to a command must be absolute, and the trainer must insist on completely accurate responses from the dog. A trainer cannot command his dog to sit and then settle for the dog's melting into the down position. Often owners are so pleased that their dogs "did something" in response to a command that they just shrug and say, "OK, down" even though they wanted the dog to sit. You want your dog to respond to the command without hesitation: he must respond at that moment and correctly every time.

READY, SIT, GO!

On your marks, get set: train! Most professional trainers agree that the sit command is the place to start your dog's formal education. Sitting is a natural posture for most dogs, and they respond to the sit exercise willingly and readily. For every lesson, begin with the sit command so that you start out with a successful exercise; likewise, you should practice the sit command at the end of every lesson as well, because you always want to end on a high note.

to catch him whenever he is about to sit and, as his backside nears the floor, say "Sit, good dog!" That's positive reinforcement and, if your timing is sharp, he will learn that what he's doing at that second is connected to your saying "Sit" and that you think he's clever for doing it!

Another method is to start with the puppy on his leash in front of you. Show him a treat in the palm of your right hand. Bring your hand up under his nose and, almost in slow motion, move your hand up and back so his nose goes up in the air and his head tilts back as he follows the treat in your hand. At that point, he will have to either sit or fall over, so as his back legs buckle under, say "Sit, good dog," and then give him the treat and lots of praise. You may have to begin with your hand lightly running up his chest, actually lifting his chin up until he sits. Some (usually older) dogs require gentle pressure on their hindquarters with the left hand, in which case the dog should be on your left side. Puppies generally do not appreciate this physical dominance.

After a few times, you should be able to show the dog a treat in the open palm of your hand, raise your hand waist-high as you say "Sit" and have him sit. You will thereby have taught him two things at the same time. Both the verbal command and the motion of the hand are signals for the sit. Your puppy is watching you almost more than he is listening to you, so what you do is just as important as what you say.

Don't save any of these drills only for training sessions. Use them as much as possible at odd times during a normal day. The dog should always sit before being given his food dish. He should sit to let you go through a doorway first, when the doorbell rings or when you stop to speak to someone on the street.

THE DOWN EXERCISE
Before beginning to teach the down command, you must consider how the dog feels about this exercise. To him, "Down" is a submissive position. Being flat on the floor with you standing over him is not his idea of fun. It's up to you to let him know that, while it may not be fun, the reward of your approval is worth his effort.

Start with the puppy on your left side in a sit position. Hold the

leash right above his collar in your left hand. Have an extra-special treat, such as a small piece of cooked chicken or hot dog, in your right hand. Place it at the end of the pup's nose and steadily move your hand down and forward along the ground. Hold the leash to prevent a sudden lunge for the food. As the puppy goes into the down position, say "Down" very gently.

The difficulty with this exercise is twofold: it's both the submissive aspect and the fact that most people say the word "Down" as if they were a drill sergeant in charge of recruits! So issue the command sweetly, give him the treat and have the pup maintain the down position for several seconds. If he tries to get up imme-

If the "treat-above-the-head" method isn't working, you may have to gently guide your Beardie into position so that he understands what's expected of him when you say "Sit."

SAY IT SIMPLY
When you command your dog to sit, use the word "Sit." Do not say "Sit down," as your dog will not know whether you mean "Sit" or "Down," or maybe you mean both. Be clear in your instructions to your dog; use one-word commands and always be consistent.

This trainer is using the hand signal for the stay: an open palm facing the dog.

diately, place your hands on his shoulders and press down gently, giving him a very quiet "Good dog." As you progress with this lesson, increase the "down time"

SMILE WHEN YOU ORDER ME AROUND!

While trainers recommend practicing with your dog every day, it's perfectly acceptable to take a "mental health day" off. It's better not to train the dog on days when you're in a sour mood. Your bad attitude or lack of interest will be sensed by your dog, and he will respond accordingly. Studies show that dogs are well-tuned-in to their humans' emotions. Be conscious of how you use your voice when talking to your dog. Raising your voice or shouting will only erode your dog's trust in you as his trainer and master.

until he will hold it until you say "Okay" (his cue for release). Practice this one in the house at various times throughout the day.

By increasing the length of time during which the dog must maintain the down position, you'll find many uses for it. For example, he can lie at your feet in the vet's office or anywhere that both of you have to wait, when you are on the phone, while the family is eating and so forth. If you progress to training for competitive obedience, he'll already be all set for the exercise called the "long down."

THE STAY EXERCISE

You can teach your Bearded Collie to stay in the sit, down and stand positions. To teach the sit/stay, have the dog sit on your left side. Hold the leash at waist level in your left hand and let the dog know that you have a treat in your closed right hand. Step forward on your right foot as you say "Stay." Immediately turn and stand directly in front of the dog, keeping your right hand up high so he'll keep his eye on the treat hand and maintain the sit position for a count of five. Return to your original position and offer the reward.

Increase the length of the sit/stay each time until the dog can hold it for at least 30 seconds without moving. After about a week of success, move out on your right foot and take two steps before turning to face the dog. Give the "Stay" hand signal (left palm back toward the dog's head) as you leave. He gets the treat when you return and he holds the sit/stay. Increase the distance that you walk away from him before turning until you reach the length of your training leash. But don't rush it! Go back to the beginning if he moves before he should. No matter what the lesson, never be upset by having to back up for a few days. The repetition and practice are what will make your dog reliable in these commands. It

won't do any good to move on to something more difficult if the command is not mastered at the easier levels. Above all, even if you do get frustrated, never let your puppy know! Always keep a positive, upbeat attitude during training, which will transmit to your dog for positive results.

The down/stay is taught in the same way once the dog is completely reliable and steady with the down command. Again, don't rush it. With the dog in the down position on your left side, step out on your right foot as you

If your Beardie becomes distracted during the lesson, take a break and try again later. You will not have success if the dog is not paying attention to you.

say "Stay." Return by walking around in back of the dog and into your original position. While you are training, it's okay to murmur something like "Hold on" to encourage him to stay put. When the dog will stay without moving when you are at a distance of 3 or 4 feet, begin to increase the length of time before you return. Be sure he holds the down on your return until you say "Okay." At that point, he gets his treat—just so he'll remember for next time that it's not over until it's over.

THE COME EXERCISE

No command is more important to the safety of your Bearded Collie than "Come." It is what you should say every single time you see the puppy running toward you: "Binky, come! Good dog." During playtime, run a few feet

---

away from the puppy and turn and tell him to "Come" as he is already running to you. You can go so far as to teach your puppy two things at once if you squat down and hold out your arms. As the pup gets close to you and you're saying "Good dog," bring your right arm in about waist high. Now he's also learning the hand signal, an excellent device should you be on the phone when you need to get him to come to you! You'll also both be one step ahead when you enter obedience classes.

When the puppy responds to your well-timed "Come," try it with the puppy on the training leash. This time, catch him off guard, while he's sniffing a leaf or watching a bird: "Binky, come!" You may have to pause for a split second after his name to be sure you have his attention. If the puppy shows any sign of confusion, give the leash a mild jerk and take a couple of steps backward. Do not repeat the command. In this case, you should say "Good come" as he reaches you.

That's the number-one rule of training. Each command word is given just once. Anything more is nagging. You'll also notice that all commands are one word only. Even when they are actually two words, you say them as one.

Never call the dog to come to you—with or without his name—if you are angry or intend to

---

OKAY!

This is the signal that tells your dog that he can quit whatever he was doing. Use "Okay" to end a session on a correct response to a command. (Never end on an incorrect response.) Lots of praise follows. People use "Okay" a lot and it has other uses for dogs, too. Your dog is barking. You say, "Okay! Come!" "Okay" signals him to stop the barking activity and "Come" allows him to come to you for a "Good dog."

correct him for some misbehavior. When correcting the pup, you go to him. Your dog must always connect "Come" with something pleasant and with your approval; then you can rely on his response.

Puppies, like children, have notoriously short attention spans, so don't overdo it with any of the training. Keep each lesson short. Break it up with a quick run around the yard or a ball toss, repeat the lesson and quit as soon as the pup gets it right. That way, you will always end with a "Good dog."

Life isn't perfect and neither are puppies. A time will come, often around ten months of age, when he'll become "selectively deaf" or choose to "forget" his name. He may respond by wagging his tail (and even seeming to smile at you) with a look that says "Make me!" Laugh, throw his favorite toy and skip the lesson you had planned. Pups will be pups!

THE HEEL EXERCISE
The second most important command to teach, after the come, is the heel. When you are walking

It is important to make teaching "Come" an enjoyable experience for your dog, as this is the most important command for your dog to learn reliably. It could save your Bearded Collie's life!

your growing puppy, you need to be in control. Besides, it looks terrible to be pulled and yanked down the street, and it's not much fun either. Your eight- to ten-week-old puppy will probably follow you everywhere, but that's his natural instinct, not your control over the situation. However, any time he does follow you, you can say "Heel" and be ahead of the game, as he will learn to associate this command with the action of following you before you even begin teaching him to heel.

There is a very precise, almost military, procedure for teaching your dog to heel. As with all other obedience training, begin with the dog on your left side. He will be in a very nice sit and you will have the training leash across your chest. Hold the loop and folded leash in your right hand. Pick up the slack leash above the dog in your left hand and hold it loosely at your side. Step out on your left foot as you say "Heel." If the puppy does not move, give a gentle tug or pat your left leg to get him started. If he surges ahead of you, stop and pull him back gently until he is at your side. Tell him to sit and begin again.

Walk a few steps and stop while the puppy is correctly beside you. Tell him to sit and give mild verbal praise. (More enthusiastic praise will encourage him to think the lesson is over.) Repeat the lesson, increasing the number of steps you take only as long as the dog is heeling nicely beside you. When you end the lesson, have him hold the sit and then give him the "Okay" to let him know that this is the end of the lesson. Praise him so that he knows he did a good job.

The cure for excessive pulling (a common problem) is to stop when the dog is no more than 2 or 3 feet ahead of you. Guide him back into position and begin again. With a really determined puller, try switching to a head collar. This will automatically turn the pup's head toward you so you can bring him back easily to the heel position. Give quiet, reassuring praise every time the leash goes slack and he's staying with you.

Staying and heeling can take a lot out of a dog, so provide playtime and free-running exercise to shake off the stress when the

LET'S GO!

Many people use "Let's go" instead of "Heel" when teaching their dogs to behave on lead. It sounds more like fun! When beginning to teach the heel, whatever command you use, always step off on your left foot. That's the one next to the dog, who is on your left side, in case you've forgotten. Keep a loose leash. When the dog pulls ahead, stop, bring him back and begin again. Use treats to guide him around turns.

lessons are over. You don't want him to associate training with all work and no fun.

TAPERING OFF TIDBITS
Your dog has been watching you—and the hand that treats—throughout all of his lessons, and now it's time to break the treat habit. Begin by giving him treats at the end of each lesson only. Then start to give a treat after the end of only some of the lessons. At the end of every lesson, as well as during the lessons, be consistent with the praise. Your pup now doesn't know whether he'll get a treat or not, but he should keep performing well just in case! Finally, you will stop giving treat rewards entirely. Save them for something brand-new that you want to teach him. Keep up the praise and you'll always have a "good dog."

OBEDIENCE CLASSES
The advantages of an obedience class are that your dog will have to learn amid the distractions of other people and dogs and that your mistakes will be quickly corrected by the trainer. Teaching your dog along with a qualified instructor and other handlers who may have more dog experience than you is another plus of the class environment. The instructor and other handlers can help you find the most efficient way of teaching your dog a command or

exercise. It's often easier to learn from other people's mistakes than your own. You will also learn all of the requirements for competitive obedience trials, in which you can earn titles and go on to advanced jumping and retrieving exercises, which are fun for many dogs. Obedience classes build the

Heeling is when the dog walks beside the owner without pulling. Once a Bearded Collie learns to heel properly, even a child could handle walking him.

foundation needed for many other canine activities (in which we humans are allowed to participate, too!).

TRAINING FOR OTHER ACTIVITIES

Once your dog has basic obedience under his collar and is 12 months of age, you can enter the world of agility training. Dogs think agility is pure fun, like being turned loose in an amusement park full of obstacles! Beardies, with their exuberance and energy, have a natural aptitude for agility work, and members of the breed have achieved high levels of success in agility.

In addition to obedience and agility, which are open to all breeds, there are specialized areas

SHOULD WE ENROLL?

If you have the means and the time, you should definitely take your dog to obedience classes. Begin with Puppy Kindergarten classes in which puppies of all sizes learn basic lessons while getting the opportunity to meet and greet each other; it's as much about socialization as it is about good manners. What you learn in class you can practice at home. And if you goof up in practice, you'll get help in the next session.

of competition geared toward certain breeds or groups. For the Beardie, this means herding tests and trials. Many owners of working and companion Beardies alike enjoy the opportunity to develop

At an agility trial, owners run through the course and give their dogs commands to guide them successfully. One of the most challenging exercises for the enthusiastic Beardie is the 30-second pause.

Agility is a high-energy sport, enjoyed by dogs, handlers and spectators. Bearded Collies have a natural aptitude for agility due to their athleticism, trainability and desire to please. This Beardie is crossing over the see-saw obstacle.

and test their dogs' instincts in this manner. Tracking is another all-breed competition open to all "nosey" dogs (which would include all dogs!). For those who like to volunteer, there is the wonderful feeling of owning a therapy dog and visiting hospitals, nursing homes and veterans' homes to bring smiles, comfort and companionship to those who are staying or living there. ·

Around the house, your Bearded Collie can be taught to do some simple chores. You might teach him to carry a basket of household items or to fetch the morning newspaper. The kids can teach the dog all kinds of tricks, from playing hide-and-seek to balancing a biscuit on his nose. A family dog is what rounds out the family. Everything he does, including sitting at your feet and gazing lovingly at you, represents the bonus of owning a dog.

This Bearded Collie sails over the bar jump at an agility trial.

HEALTHCARE OF YOUR
BEARDED COLLIE

By Lowell Ackerman, DVM, DACVD

HEALTHCARE FOR A LIFETIME

When you own a dog, you become his healthcare advocate over his entire lifespan, as well as being the one to shoulder the financial burden of such care. Accordingly, it is worthwhile to focus on prevention rather than treatment, as you and your pet will both be happier.

Of course, the best place to have begun your program of preventive healthcare is with the initial purchase or adoption of your dog. There is no way of guaranteeing that your new furry friend is free of medical problems, but there are some things you can do to improve your odds. You certainly should have done adequate research into the Bearded Collie and have selected your puppy carefully rather than buying on impulse. Health issues aside, a large number of pet abandonment

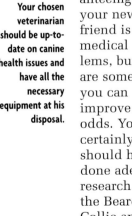

Your chosen veterinarian should be up-to-date on canine health issues and have all the necessary equipment at his disposal.

and relinquishment cases arise from a mismatch between pet needs and owner expectations. This is entirely preventable with appropriate planning and finding a good breeder.

Regarding healthcare issues specifically, it is very difficult to make blanket statements about where to acquire a problem-free pet, but, again, a reputable breeder is your best bet. In an ideal situation, you have the opportunity to see both parents, get references from other owners of the breeder's pups and see genetic-testing documentation for several generations of the litter's ancestors. At the very least, you must thoroughly investigate your breed of interest and the problems inherent in that breed, as well as the genetic testing available to screen for those problems. Genetic testing offers some important benefits, but testing is available for only a few disorders in a relatively small number of breeds and is not available for some of the most common genetic diseases, such as hip dysplasia, cataracts, epilepsy, cardiomyopathy, etc. This area of research is indeed exciting and increasingly important, and advances will continue to be made each year. In fact, recent research has shown that there is an equivalent dog gene for 75% of known human genes, so research done in either species is likely to benefit the other.

We've also discussed that evaluating the behavioral nature of your Bearded Collie and that of his immediate family members is an important part of the selection process that cannot be underestimated or overemphasized. It is sometimes difficult to evaluate temperament in puppies because certain behavioral tendencies, such as some forms of aggression, may not be immediately evident. More dogs are euthanized each year for behavioral reasons than for all medical conditions combined, so it is critical to take temperament issues seriously. Start with a well-balanced, friendly companion and put the time and effort into proper socialization, and you will both be rewarded with a valued relationship for the life of the dog.

Assuming that you have started off with a pup from healthy, sound stock, you then become responsible for helping your veterinarian keep your pet healthy. Some crucial things happen before you even bring your puppy home. Parasite control typically begins at two weeks of age, and vaccinations typically begin at six to eight weeks of age. A pre-pubertal evaluation is typically scheduled for about six months of age. At this

TAKING YOUR DOG'S TEMPERATURE

It is important to know how to take your dog's temperature at times when you think he may be ill. It's not the most enjoyable task, but it can be done without too much difficulty. It's easier with a helper, preferably someone with whom the dog is friendly, so that one of you can hold the dog while the other inserts the thermometer.

Before inserting the thermometer, coat the end with petroleum jelly. Insert the thermometer slowly and gently into the dog's rectum about one inch. Wait for the reading—digital thermometers will register in less than a minute. Be sure to remove the thermometer carefully and clean it thoroughly after each use.

A dog's normal body temperature is between 100.5 and 102.5 degrees F. Immediate veterinary attention is required if the dog's temperature is below 99 or above 104 degrees F.

time, a dental evaluation is done (since the adult teeth are now in), heartworm prevention is started and neutering or spaying is most commonly done.

It is critical to commence regular dental care at home if you have not already done so. It may not sound very important, but most dogs have active periodontal disease by four years of age if they don't have their teeth cleaned regularly at home, not just at their veterinary exams. Dental problems lead to more than just bad "doggie breath." Gum disease can have very serious medical consequences. If you start brushing your dog's teeth and using antiseptic rinses from a young age, your dog will be accustomed to it and will not resist. The results will be healthy dentition, which your pet will need to enjoy a long, healthy life.

DOGGIE DENTAL DON'TS

A veterinary dental exam is necessary if you notice one or any combination of the following in your dog:

- Broken, loose or missing teeth
- Loss of appetite (which could be due to mouth pain or illness caused by infection)
- Gum abnormalities, including redness, swelling and bleeding
- Drooling, with or without blood
- Yellowing of the teeth or gumline, indicating tartar
- Bad breath

Most dogs are considered adults at a year of age, although some Beardies may have some filling out to do up to about two or so years old. Even individual dogs within each breed have different healthcare requirements, so work with your veterinarian to determine what will be needed and what your role should be. This doctor-client relationship is important, because as vaccination guidelines change, there may not be an annual "vaccine visit" scheduled. You must make sure that you see your veterinarian at least annually, even if no vaccines are due, because this is the best opportunity to coordinate healthcare activities and to make sure that no medical issues creep by unaddressed.

When your Bearded Collie reaches about three-quarters of his anticipated lifespan, he is considered a "senior" and will require some special care whether or not he is showing signs of aging. In general, if you've been taking great care of your canine companion throughout his formative and adult years, the transition to senior status should be a smooth one. Age is not a disease, and as long as everything is functioning as it should, there is no reason why most of late adulthood should not be rewarding for both you and your pet. This is especially true if you have tended to the details, such as regular veterinary visits, proper dental care, excellent nutrition and management of bone and joint issues.

At this stage in your Bearded Collie's life, your veterinarian will schedule visits twice yearly, instead of once, to run some laboratory screenings, electrocardiograms and the like, and to change the diet to something more digestible. Catching problems early is the best way to manage them effectively. Treating the early stages of heart disease is so much easier than trying to intervene when there is more significant damage to the heart muscle. Similarly, managing the beginning of kidney problems is fairly routine if there is no significant kidney damage. Other problems, like cognitive dysfunction (similar to senility and Alzheimer's disease), cancer, diabetes and arthritis, are more common in older dogs, but all can be treated to help the dog live as many happy, comfortable years as possible. Just as in people, medical management is more effective (and less expensive) when you catch things early.

SELECTING A VETERINARIAN

There is probably no more important decision that you will make regarding your pet's healthcare than the selection of his doctor. Your pet's veterinarian will be a pediatrician, family-practice physician and gerontologist, depending on the dog's life stage, and will be the individual who makes recom-

PROBLEM: AND THAT STARTS WITH "P"

Urinary tract problems more commonly affect female dogs, especially those who have been spayed. The first sign that a urinary tract problem exists usually is a strong odor from the urine or an unusual color. Blood in the urine, known as hematuria, is another sign of an infection, related to cystitis, a bladder infection, bladder cancer or a blood-clotting disorder. Urinary tract problems can also be signaled by the dog's straining while urinating, experiencing pain during urination and genital discharge as well as excessive water intake and urination.

Excessive drinking, in and of itself, does not indicate a urinary tract problem. A dog who is drinking more than normal may have a kidney or liver problem, a hormonal disorder or diabetes mellitus. Behaviorists report a disorder known as psychogenic polydipsia, which manifests itself in excessive drinking and urination. If you notice your dog drinking much more than normal, take him to the vet.

mendations regarding issues such as when specialists need to be consulted, when diagnostic testing and/or therapeutic intervention is needed and when you will need to seek outside emergency and critical-care services. Your vet will act as your advocate and liaison throughout these processes.

YOUR DOG NEEDS TO VISIT THE VET IF:

- He has ingested a toxin such as antifreeze or a toxic plant; in these cases, administer first aid and call the vet right away
- His teeth are discolored, loose or missing or he has sores or other signs of infection or abnormality in the mouth
- He has been vomiting, has had diarrhea or has been constipated for over 24 hours; call immediately if you notice blood
- He has refused food for over 24 hours
- His eating habits, water intake or toilet habits have noticeably changed; if you have noticed weight gain or weight loss
- He shows symptoms of bloat, which requires *immediate* attention
- He is salivating excessively
- He has a lump in his throat
- He has lumps or bumps anywhere on the body
- He is very lethargic
- He appears to be in pain or otherwise has trouble chewing or swallowing
- His skin loses elasticity

Of course, there will be other instances in which a visit to the vet is necessary; these are just some of the signs that could be indicative of serious problems that need to be caught as early as possible.

Everyone has his own idea about what to look for in a vet, an individual who will play a big role in his dog's (and, of course, his own) life for many years to come. For some, it is the compassionate caregiver with whom they hope to develop a professional relationship to span the lifetime of their dogs and even their future pets. For others, they are seeking a clinician with keen diagnostic and therapeutic insight who can deliver state-of-the-art healthcare. Still others need a veterinary facility that is open evenings and weekends, or is in close proximity or provides mobile veterinary services, to accommodate their schedules; these people may not much mind that their dogs might see different veterinarians on each visit. Just as we have different reasons for selecting our own healthcare professionals (e.g., covered by insurance plan, expert in field, convenient location, etc.), we should not expect that there is a one-size-fits-all recommendation for selecting a veterinarian and veterinary practice. The best advice is to be honest in your assessment of what you expect from a veterinary practice and to conscientiously research the options in your area. You will quickly appreciate that not all veterinary practices are the same, and you will be happiest with one that truly meets your needs.

There is another point to be considered in the selection of veterinary services. Not that long ago, a single veterinarian would attempt to manage all medical and surgical issues as they arose. That was often problematic because veterinarians are trained in many species and many diseases, and it was just impossible for general veterinary practitioners to be experts in every species, every field and every ailment. However, just as in the human healthcare fields, specialization has allowed general practitioners to concentrate on primary healthcare delivery, especially wellness and the prevention of infectious diseases, and to utilize a network of specialists to assist in the management of conditions that require specific expertise and experience. Thus there are now many types of veterinary specialists, including dermatologists, cardiologists, ophthalmologists, surgeons, internists, oncologists, neurologists, behaviorists, criticalists and others to help primary-care veterinarians deal with complicated medical challenges. In most cases, specialists see cases referred by primary-care veterinarians, make diagnoses and set up management plans. From there, the animal's ongoing care is returned to his primary-care veterinarians. This important team approach to your pet's

As much as your Bearded Collie loves to be outside, you must make sure that he is properly protected from fleas, ticks and other parasites so you both can enjoy outdoor playtime worry-free.

medical-care needs has provided opportunities for advanced care and an unparalleled level of quality to be delivered.

With all of the opportunities for your Bearded Collie to receive high-quality veterinary medical care, there is another topic that needs to be addressed at the same time—cost. It's been said that you can have excellent healthcare or inexpensive healthcare, but never both; this is as true in veterinary medicine as it is in human medicine. While veterinary costs are a fraction of what the same services cost in the human healthcare arena, it is still difficult to deal with unanticipated medical costs, especially since they can easily creep into hundreds or even thousands of dollars if specialists or emergency services become involved. However, there are ways of managing these risks. The easiest is to buy pet health insurance and realize that its foremost purpose is not to cover routine healthcare visits but rather to serve as an umbrella for those rainy days when your pet needs medical care and you don't want to worry about whether or not you can afford that care.

Pet insurance policies are very cost-effective (and very inexpensive by human health-insurance standards), but make sure that you buy the policy long before you intend to use it (preferably starting in puppyhood, because cover-age will exclude pre-existing conditions) and that you are actually buying an indemnity insurance plan from an insurance company that is regulated by your state or province. Many insurance policy look-alikes are actually discount clubs that are redeemable only at specific locations and for specific services. An indemnity plan covers your pet at almost all veterinary, specialty and emergency practices and is an excellent way to manage your pet's ongoing healthcare needs.

VACCINATIONS AND INFECTIOUS DISEASES

There has never been an easier time to prevent a variety of infectious diseases in your dog, but the advances we've made in veterinary medicine come with a price—choice. Now while it may seem that choice is a good thing (and it is), it has never been more difficult for the pet owner (or the veterinarian) to make an informed decision about the best way to protect pets through vaccination.

Years ago, it was just accepted that puppies got a starter series of vaccinations and then annual "boosters" throughout their lives to keep them protected. As more and more vaccines became available, consumers wanted the convenience of having all of that protection in a single injection. The result was "multivalent" vaccines that crammed a lot of

COMMON INFECTIOUS DISEASES

Let's discuss some of the diseases that create the need for vaccination in the first place. Following are the major canine infectious diseases and a simple explanation of each.

Rabies: A devastating viral disease that can be fatal in dogs and people. In fact, vaccination of dogs and cats is an important public-health measure to create a resistant animal buffer population to protect people from contracting the disease. Vaccination schedules are determined on a government level and are not optional for pet owners; rabies vaccination is required by law in all 50 states.

Parvovirus: A severe, potentially life-threatening disease that is easily transmitted between dogs. There are four strains of the virus, but it is believed that there is significant "cross-protection" between strains that may be included in individual vaccines.

Distemper: A potentially severe and life-threatening disease with a relatively high risk of exposure, especially in certain regions. In very high-risk distemper environments, young pups may be vaccinated with human measles vaccine, a related virus that offers cross-protection when administered at four to ten weeks of age.

Hepatitis: Caused by canine adenovirus type 1 (CAV-1), but since vaccination with the causative virus has a higher rate of adverse effects, cross-protection is derived from the use of adenovirus type 2 (CAV-2), a cause of respiratory disease and one of the potential causes of canine cough. Vaccination with CAV-2 provides long-term immunity against hepatitis but relatively less protection against respiratory infection.

Canine cough: Also called tracheobronchitis, actually a fairly complicated result of viral and bacterial offenders; therefore, even with vaccination, protection is incomplete. Wherever dogs congregate, canine cough will likely be spread among them. Intranasal vaccination with *Bordetella* and parainfluenza is the best safeguard, but the duration of immunity does not appear to be very long, typically a year at most. These are non-core vaccines, but vaccination is sometimes mandated by boarding kennels, obedience classes, dog shows and other places where dogs congregate to try to minimize spread of infection.

Leptospirosis: A potentially fatal disease that is more common in some geographic regions. It is capable of being spread to humans. The disease varies with the individual "serovar," or strain, of *Leptospira* involved. Since there does not appear to be much cross-protection between serovars, protection is only as good as the likelihood that the serovar in the vaccine is the same as the one in the pet's local environment. Problems with *Leptospira* vaccines are that protection does not last very long, side effects are not uncommon and a large percentage of dogs (perhaps 30%) may not respond to vaccination.

Borrelia burgdorferi: The cause of Lyme disease, the risk of which varies with the geographic area in which the pet lives and travels. Lyme disease is spread by deer ticks in the eastern US and western black-legged ticks in the western part of the country, and the risk of exposure is high in some regions. Lameness, fever and inappetence are most commonly seen in affected dogs. The extent of protection from the vaccine has not been conclusively demonstrated.

Coronavirus: This disease has a high risk of exposure, especially in areas where dogs congregate, but it typically causes only mild to moderate digestive upset (diarrhea, vomiting, etc.). Vaccines are available, but the duration of protection is believed to be relatively short and the effectiveness of the vaccine in preventing infection is considered low.

There are many other vaccinations available, including those for *Giardia* and canine adenovirus-1. While there may be some specific indications for their use, and local risk factors to be considered, they are not widely recommended for most dogs.

protection into a single syringe. The manufacturers' recommendations were to give the vaccines annually, and this was a simple enough protocol to follow. However, as veterinary medicine has become more sophisticated and we have started looking more at healthcare quandaries rather than convenience, it became necessary to reevaluate the situation and deal with some tough questions.

It is important to realize that whether or not to use a particular vaccine depends on the risk of contracting the disease against which it protects, the severity of the disease if it is contracted, the duration of immunity provided by the vaccine, the safety of the product and the needs of the individual animal. In a very general sense, rabies, distemper, hepatitis and parvovirus are considered core vaccine needs, while parainfluenza, *Bordetella bronchiseptica*, leptospirosis, coronavirus and borreliosis (Lyme disease) are considered non-core needs and best reserved for animals that demonstrate reasonable risk of contracting the diseases.

NEUTERING/SPAYING
Sterilization procedures (neutering for males/spaying for females) are meant to accomplish several purposes. While the underlying premise is to address the risk of pet overpopulation, there are also

The Beardie can be susceptible to skin and coat problems, like allergies of various types. A grass or pollen allergy can be the cause of your Beardie's excessive scratching.

some medical and behavioral benefits to the surgeries as well. For females, spaying prior to the first estrus (heat cycle) leads to a marked reduction in the risk of mammary cancer. There also will be no manifestations of "heat" to attract male dogs and no bleeding in the house. For males, there is prevention of testicular cancer and a reduction in the risk of prostate problems. In both sexes, there may be some limited reduction in aggressive behaviors

toward other dogs, and some diminishing of urine marking, roaming and mounting.

While neutering and spaying do indeed prevent animals from contributing to pet overpopulation, even no-cost and low-cost neutering options have not eliminated the problem. Perhaps one of the main reasons for this is that individuals that intentionally breed their dogs and those that allow their animals to run at large are the main causes of unwanted offspring. Also, animals in shelters are often there because they were abandoned or relinquished, not because they came from unplanned matings. Neutering/spaying is important, but it should be considered in the context of the real causes of animals' ending up in shelters and eventually being euthanized.

One of the important considerations regarding neutering is that it is a surgical procedure. This sometimes gets lost in discussions of low-cost procedures and commoditization of the process. In females, spaying is specifically referred to as an ovariohysterectomy. In this procedure, a midline incision is made in the abdomen and the entire uterus and both ovaries are surgically removed. While this is a major invasive surgical procedure, it usually has few complications because it is typically performed on healthy young animals. However, it is major surgery, as any woman who has had a hysterectomy will attest.

In males, neutering has traditionally referred to castration, which involves the surgical removal of both testicles. While still a significant piece of surgery, there is not the abdominal exposure that is required in the female surgery. In addition, there is now a chemical sterilization option, in which a solution is injected into each testicle, leading to atrophy of the sperm-producing cells. This can typically be done under sedation rather than full anesthesia. This is a relatively new approach, and there are no long-term clinical studies yet available.

Neutering/spaying is typically done around six months of age at most veterinary hospitals, although techniques have been pioneered to perform the procedures in animals as young as eight weeks of age. In general, the surgeries on the very young animals are done for the specific reason of sterilizing them before they go to their new homes. This is done in some shelter hospitals for assurance that the animals will definitely not produce any pups. Otherwise, these organizations need to rely on owners to comply with their wishes to have the animals "altered" at a later date, something that does not always happen.

A scanning electron micrograph of a dog flea, *Ctenocephalides canis*, on dog hair.

EXTERNAL PARASITES

FLEAS

Fleas have been around for millions of years and, while we have better tools now for controlling them than at any time in the past, there still is little chance that they will end up on an endangered species list. Actually, they are very well adapted to living on our pets, and they continue to adapt as we make advances.

The female flea can consume 15 times her weight in blood during active reproduction and can lay as many as 40 eggs a day. These eggs are very resistant to the effects of insecticides. They hatch into larvae, which then mature and spin cocoons. The immature fleas reside in this pupal stage until the time is right for feeding. This pupal stage is also very resistant to the effects of insecticides, and pupae can last in the environment without feeding for many months. Newly emergent fleas are attracted to animals by the warmth of the animals' bodies, movement and exhaled carbon dioxide. However, when they first emerge from their cocoons, they orient towards light; thus when an animal passes between a flea and the light source, casting a shadow, the flea pounces and starts to feed. If the animal turns out to be a dog or cat, the reproductive cycle continues. If the flea lands on another type of animal, including a person, the flea will bite but will then look for a more appropriate host. An emerging adult flea can survive without feeding for up to 12 months, but once it tastes blood it can survive off its host for only three to four days.

It was once thought that fleas spend most of their lives in the environment, but we now know that fleas won't willingly jump off a dog unless leaping to another dog or when physically removed by brushing, bathing or other manipulation. Flea eggs, on the other hand, are shiny and smooth, and they roll off the animal and into the environment. The eggs, larvae and pupae then exist in the environment, but once the adult finds a susceptible animal, it's home sweet home until the flea is forced to seek refuge elsewhere.

Since adult fleas live on the animal and immature forms survive in the environment, a successful treatment plan must address all stages of the flea life cycle. There are now several safe and effective flea-control products that can be applied on a monthly

FLEA PREVENTION FOR YOUR DOG
- Discuss with your veterinarian the safest product to protect your dog, likely in the form of a monthly tablet or a liquid preparation placed on the back of the dog's neck.
- For dogs suffering from flea-bite dermatitis, a shampoo or topical insecticide treatment is required.
- Your lawn and property should be sprayed with an insecticide designed to kill fleas and ticks that lurk outdoors.
- Using a flea comb, check the dog's coat regularly for any signs of parasites.
- Practice good housekeeping. Vacuum floors, carpets and furniture regularly, especially in the areas that the dog frequents, and wash the dog's bedding weekly.
- Follow up house-cleaning with carpet shampoos and sprays to rid the house of fleas at all stages of development. Insect growth regulators are the safest option.

basis. These include fipronil, imidacloprid, selamectin and permethrin (found in several formulations). Most of these products have significant flea-killing rates within 24 hours. However, none of them will control the immature forms in the environment. To accomplish this, there are a variety of insect growth regulators that can be sprayed into

THE FLEA'S LIFE CYCLE

What came first, the flea or the egg? This age-old mystery is more difficult to comprehend than the actual cycle of the flea. Fleas usually live only about four months. A female can lay 2,000 eggs in her lifetime.

PHOTO BY CAROLINA BIOLOGICAL SUPPLY CO.

Egg

After ten days of rolling around your carpet or under your furniture, the eggs hatch into larvae, which feed on various and sundry debris. In days or months, depending on the climate, the larvae spin cocoons and develop into the pupal or nymph stage, which quickly develop into fleas.

Larva

PHOTO BY CAROLINA BIOLOGICAL SUPPLY CO.

Pupa

These immature fleas must locate a host within 10 to 14 days or they will die. Only about 1% of the flea population exist as adult fleas, while the other 99% exist as eggs, larvae or pupae.

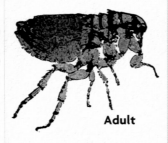

Adult

KILL FLEAS THE NATURAL WAY

If you choose not to go the route of conventional medication, there are some natural ways to ward off fleas:
- Dust your dog with a natural flea powder, composed of such herbal goodies as rosemary, wormwood, pennyroyal, citronella, rue, tobacco powder and eucalyptus.
- Apply diatomaceous earth, the fossilized remains of single-cell algae, to your carpets, furniture and pet's bedding. Even though it's not good for dogs, it's even worse for fleas, which will dry up swiftly and die.
- Brush your dog frequently, give him adequate exercise and let him fast occasionally. All of these activities strengthen the dog's system and make him more resistant to disease and parasites.
- Bathe your dog with a capful of pennyroyal or eucalyptus oil.
- Feed a natural diet, free of additives and preservatives. Add some fresh garlic and brewer's yeast to the dog's morning portion, as these items have flea-repelling properties.

the environment (e.g., pyriprox-yfen, methoprene, fenoxycarb) as well as insect development inhibitors such as lufenuron that can be administered. These compounds have no effect on adult fleas, but they stop imma-ture forms from developing into adults. In years gone by, we relied heavily on toxic insecticides (such as organophosphates, organochlo-rines and carbamates) to manage the flea problem, but today's options are not only much safer to use on our pets but also safer for the environment.

TICKS

Ticks are members of the spider class (arachnids) and are blood-sucking parasites capable of transmitting a variety of diseases, including Lyme disease, ehrlichiosis, babesiosis and Rocky Mountain spotted fever. It's easy to see ticks on your own skin, but it is more of a challenge when your Bearded Collie is affected. Whenever you happen to be planning a stroll in a tick-infested area (especially forests, grassy or wooded areas or parks) be prepared to do a thorough inspection of your dog afterward to search for ticks. Ticks can be tricky, so make sure you spend time looking in the ears, between the toes and every-where else where a tick might hide. Ticks need to be attached for 24–72 hours before they transmit most of the diseases that they carry, so you do have a window of opportunity for some preventive intervention.

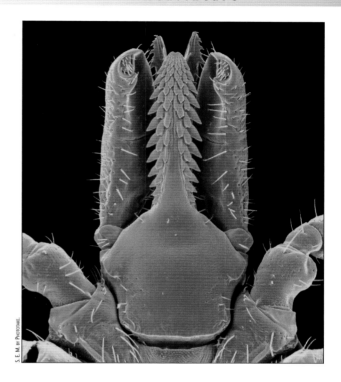

S. E. M. BY PHOTOTAKE.

A scanning electron micrograph of the head of a female deer tick, *Ixodes dammini*, a parasitic tick that carries Lyme disease.

A TICKING BOMB

There is nothing good about a tick's harpooning his nose into your dog's skin. Among the diseases caused by ticks are Rocky Mountain spotted fever, canine ehrlichiosis, canine babesiosis, canine hepatozoonosis and Lyme disease. If a dog is allergic to the saliva of a female wood tick, he can develop tick paralysis.

Female ticks live to eat and breed. They can lay between 4,000 and 5,000 eggs and they die soon after. Males, on the other hand, live only to mate with the females and continue the process as long as they are able. Most ticks live on multiple hosts before parasitizing dogs. The immature forms typically reside on grass and shrubs, waiting for suscepti-ble animals to walk by. The larvae and nymph stages typically feed on wildlife.

If only a few ticks are present on a dog, they can be plucked out, but it is important to remove the entire head and mouthparts,

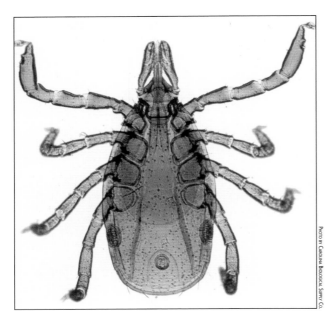

Photo by Carolina Biological Supply Co.

Deer tick,
Ixodes dammini.

which may be deeply embedded in the skin. This is best accomplished with forceps designed especially for this purpose; fingers can be used but should be protected with rubber gloves, plastic wrap or at least a paper towel. The tick should be grasped as closely as possible to the animal's skin and should be pulled upward with steady, even pressure. Do not squeeze, crush or puncture the body of the tick or you risk exposure to any disease carried by that tick. Once the ticks have been removed, the sites of attachment should be disinfected. Your hands should then be washed with soap and water to further minimize risk of contagion. The tick should be disposed

of in a container of alcohol or household bleach.

Some of the newer flea products, specifically those with fipronil, selamectin and permethrin, have effect against some, but not all, species of tick. Flea collars containing appropriate pesticides (e.g., propoxur, chlorfenvinphos) can aid in tick control. In most areas, such collars should be placed on animals in March, at the beginning of the tick season, and changed regularly. Leaving the collar on when the pesticide level is waning invites the development of resistance. Amitraz collars are also good for tick control, and the active ingredient does not interfere with other flea-control products. The ingredient helps prevent the attachment of ticks to the skin and will cause those ticks already on the skin to detach themselves.

TICK CONTROL

Removal of underbrush and leaf litter and the thinning of trees in areas where tick control is desired are recommended. These actions remove the cover and food sources for small animals that serve as hosts for ticks. With continued mowing of grasses in these areas, the probability of ticks' surviving is further reduced. A variety of insecticide ingredients (e.g., resmethrin, carbaryl, permethrin, chlorpyrifos, dioxathion and allethrin) are registered for tick control around the home.

MITES

Mites are tiny arachnid parasites that parasitize the skin of dogs. Skin diseases caused by mites are referred to as "mange," and there are many different forms seen in dogs. These forms are very different from one another, each one warranting an individual description.

Sarcoptic mange, or scabies, is one of the itchiest conditions that affects dogs. The microscopic *Sarcoptes* mites burrow into the superficial layers of the skin and can drive dogs crazy with itchiness. They are also communicable to people, although they can't complete their reproductive cycle on people. In addition to being tiny, the mites also are often difficult to find when trying to make a diagnosis. Skin scrapings from multiple areas are examined microscopically but, even then, sometimes the mites cannot be found.

Fortunately, scabies is relatively easy to treat, and there are a variety of products that will successfully kill the mites. Since the mites can't live in the environment for very long without feeding, a complete cure is usually possible within four to eight weeks.

Cheyletiellosis is caused by a relatively large mite, which sometimes can be seen even without a microscope. Often referred to as "walking dandruff," this also causes itching, but not usually as profound as with scabies. While *Cheyletiella*

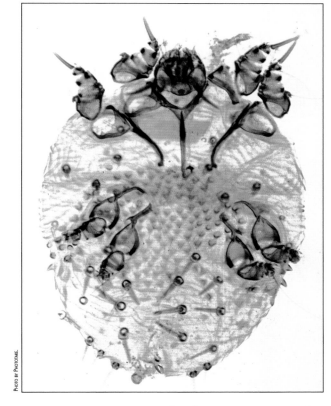

PHOTO BY PHOTOTAKE.

mites can survive somewhat longer in the environment than scabies mites, they too are relatively easy to treat, being responsive to not only the medications used to treat scabies but also often to flea-control products.

Otodectes cynotis is the canine ear mite and is one of the more common causes of mange, especially in young dogs in shelters or pet stores. That's because the mites are typically present in large numbers and are quickly spread to nearby animals. The mites rarely do

Sarcoptes scabiei, commonly known as the "itch mite."

Micrograph of a dog louse, *Heterodoxus spiniger*. Female lice attach their eggs to the hairs of the dog. As the eggs hatch, the larval lice bite and feed on the blood. Lice can also feed on dead skin and hair. This feeding activity can cause hair loss and skin problems.

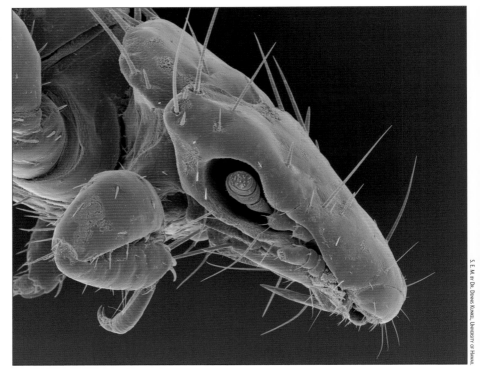

much harm but can be difficult to eradicate if the treatment regimen is not comprehensive. While many try to treat the condition with ear drops only, this is the most common cause of treatment failure. Ear drops cause the mites to simply move out of the ears and as far away as possible (usually to the base of the tail) until the insecticide levels in the ears drop to an acceptable level—then it's back to business as usual! The successful treatment of ear mites requires treating all animals in the household with a systemic insecticide, such as selamectin, or a combination of miticidal ear drops combined with whole-body flea-control preparations.

Demodicosis, sometimes referred to as red mange, can be one of the most difficult forms of mange to treat. Part of the problem has to do with the fact that the mites live in the hair follicles and they are relatively well shielded from topical and systemic products. The main issue, however, is that demodectic mange typically results only when there is some underlying process interfering with the dog's immune system.

Since *Demodex* mites are normal residents of the skin of

mammals, including humans, there is usually a mite population explosion only when the immune system fails to keep the number of mites in check. In young animals, the immune deficit may be transient or may reflect an actual inherited immune problem. In older animals, demodicosis is usually seen only when there is another disease hampering the immune system, such as diabetes, cancer, thyroid problems or the use of immune-suppressing drugs. Accordingly, treatment involves not only trying to kill the mange mites but also discerning what is interfering with immune function and correcting it if possible.

Chiggers represent several different species of mite that don't parasitize dogs specifically, but do latch on to passersby and can cause irritation. The problem is most prevalent in wooded areas in the late summer and fall. Treatment is not difficult, as the mites do not complete their life cycle on dogs and are susceptible to a variety of miticidal products.

MOSQUITOES

Mosquitoes have long been known to transmit a variety of diseases to people, as well as just being biting pests during warm weather. They also pose a real risk to pets. Not only do they carry deadly heartworms but

recently there also has been much concern over their involvement with West Nile virus. While we can avoid heartworm with the use of preventive medications, there are no such preventives for West Nile virus. The only method of prevention in endemic areas is active mosquito control. Fortunately, most dogs that have been exposed to the virus only developed flu-like symptoms and, to date, there have not been the large number of reported deaths in canines as seen in some other species.

Illustration of *Demodex folliculoram.*

ILLUSTRATION BY PHOTOTAKE.

MOSQUITO REPELLENT

Low concentrations of DEET (less than 10%), found in many human mosquito repellents, have been safely used in dogs but, in these concentrations, probably give only about two hours of protection. DEET may be safe in these small concentrations, but since it is not licensed for use on dogs, there is no research proving its safety for dogs. Products containing permethrin give the longest-lasting protection, perhaps two to four weeks. As DEET is not licensed for use on dogs, and both DEET and permethrin can be quite toxic to cats, appropriate care should be exercised. Other products, such as those containing oil of citronella, also have some mosquito-repellent activity, but typically have a relatively short duration of action.

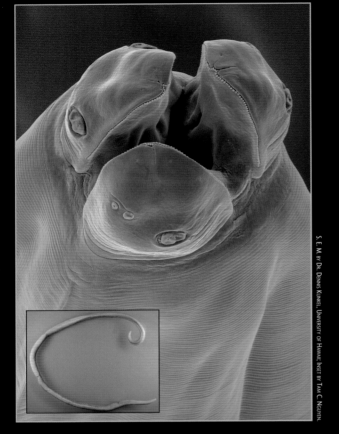

S. E. M. by Dr. Dennis Kunkel, University of Hawaii. Inset by Tam C. Nguyen.

The ascarid roundworm *Toxocara canis*, showing the mouth with three lips. INSET: Photomicrograph of the roundworm *Ascaris lumbricoides*.

INTERNAL PARASITES: WORMS

ASCARIDS

Ascarids are intestinal roundworms that rarely cause severe disease in dogs. Nonetheless, they are of major public health significance because they can be transferred to people. Sadly, it is children who are most commonly affected by the parasite, probably from inadvertently ingesting ascarid-contaminated soil. In fact, many yards and children's sand-boxes contain appreciable numbers of ascarid eggs. So, while ascarids don't bite dogs or latch onto their intestines to suck blood, they do cause some nasty medical conditions in children and are best eradicated from our furry friends. Because pups can start passing ascarid eggs by three weeks of age, most parasite-control programs begin at two weeks of age and are repeated every two weeks until pups are eight weeks old. It is important to

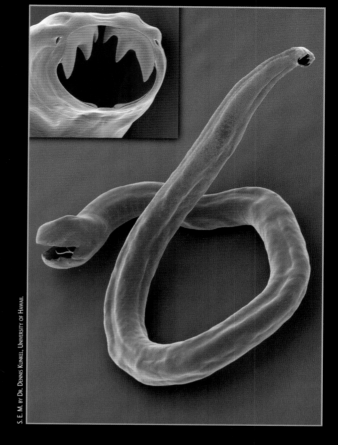

S. E. M. BY DR. DENNIS KUNKEL, UNIVERSITY OF HAWAII.

realize that bitches can pass ascarids to their pups even if they test negative prior to whelping. Accordingly, bitches are best treated at the same time as the pups.

HOOKWORMS

Unlike ascarids, hookworms do latch onto a dog's intestinal tract and can cause significant loss of blood and protein. Similar to ascarids, hookworms can be transmitted to humans, where they cause a condition known as cutaneous larval migrans. Dogs can become infected either by consuming the infective larvae or by the larvae's penetrating the skin directly. People most often get infected when they are lying on the ground (such as on a beach) and the larvae penetrate the skin. Yes, the larvae can penetrate through a beach blanket. Hookworms are typically susceptible to the same medications used to treat ascarids.

The hookworm *Ancylostoma caninum* infests the intestines of dogs. INSET: Note the row of hooks at the posterior end, used to anchor the worm to the intestinal wall.

WHIPWORMS

Whipworms latch onto the lower aspects of the dog's colon and can cause cramping and diarrhea. Eggs do not start to appear in the dog's feces until about three months after the dog was infected. This worm has a peculiar life cycle, which makes it more difficult to control than ascarids or hookworms. The good thing is that whipworms rarely are transferred to people.

Some of the medications used to treat ascarids and hookworms are also effective against whipworms, but, in general, a separate treatment protocol is needed. Since most of the medications are effective against the adults but not the eggs or larvae, treatment is typically repeated in three weeks, and then often in three

Adult whipworm, *Trichuris* sp., an intestinal parasite.

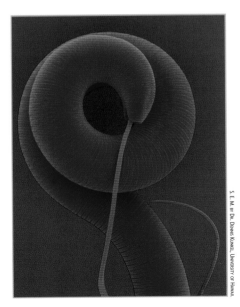

S. E. M. BY DR. DENNIS KUNKEL, UNIVERSITY OF HAWAII

WORM-CONTROL GUIDELINES

- Practice sanitary habits with your dog and home.
- Clean up after your dog and don't let him sniff or eat other dogs' droppings.
- Control insects and fleas in the dog's environment. Fleas, lice, cockroaches, beetles, mice and rats can act as hosts for various worms.
- Prevent dogs from eating uncooked meat, raw poultry and dead animals.
- Keep dogs and children from playing in sand and soil.
- Kennel dogs on cement or gravel; avoid dirt runs.
- Administer heartworm preventives regularly.
- Have your vet examine your dog's stools at your annual visits.
- Select a boarding kennel carefully so as to avoid contamination from other dogs or an unsanitary environment.
- Prevent dogs from roaming. Obey local leash laws.

months as well. Unfortunately, since dogs don't develop resistance to whipworms, it is difficult to prevent them from getting reinfected if they visit soil contaminated with whipworm eggs.

TAPEWORMS

There are many different species of tapeworm that affect dogs, but *Dipylidium caninum* is probably the most common and is spread by fleas. Flea larvae feed on organic debris and tapeworm eggs in the environment and, when a dog chews at himself and manages to ingest fleas, he might get a dose of tapeworm at the same time. The tapeworm then develops further in the intestine of the dog.

The tapeworm itself, which is a parasitic flatworm that latches onto the intestinal wall, is composed of numerous segments. When the segments break off into the intestine (as proglottids), they may accumulate around the rectum, like grains of rice. While this tapeworm is disgusting in its behavior, it is not directly communicable to humans (although humans can also get infected by swallowing fleas).

A much more dangerous flatworm is *Echinococcus multilocularis*, which is typically found in foxes, coyotes and wolves. The eggs are passed in the feces and infect rodents, and, when dogs eat the rodents, the dogs can be infected by thousands of adult tapeworms. While the parasites don't cause many problems in dogs, this is considered the most lethal worm infection that people can get. Take appropriate precautions if you live in an area in which these tapeworms are found. Do not use mulch that may contain feces of dogs, cats or wildlife, and discourage your pets from hunting

S. E. M. BY DR. DENNIS KUNKEL, UNIVERSITY OF HAWAII.

wildlife. Treat these tapeworm infections aggressively in pets, because if humans get infected, approximately half die.

HEARTWORMS

Heartworm disease is caused by the parasite *Dirofilaria immitis* and is seen in dogs around the world. A member of the roundworm group, it is spread between dogs by the bite of an infected mosquito. The mosquito injects infective larvae into the dog's skin with its bite, and these larvae develop under the skin for a period of time before making their way to the heart. There they develop into adults, which grow and create blockages of the heart, lungs and major blood vessels there. They also start producing offspring (microfilariae)

A dog tapeworm proglottid (body segment).

The dog tapeworm *Taenia pisiformis*.

S. E. M. BY DR. DENNIS KUNKEL, UNIVERSITY OF HAWAII.

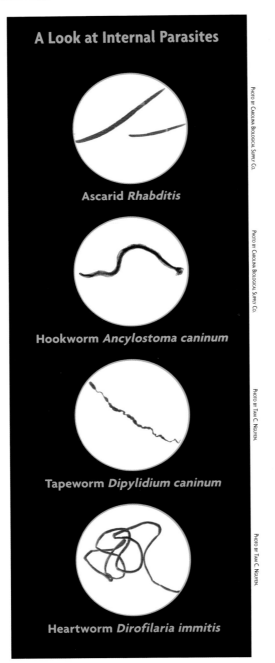

A Look at Internal Parasites

Ascarid *Rhabditis*

Hookworm *Ancylostoma caninum*

Tapeworm *Dipylidium caninum*

Heartworm *Dirofilaria immitis*

PHOTO BY CAROLINA BIOLOGICAL SUPPLY CO.

PHOTO BY CAROLINA BIOLOGICAL SUPPLY CO.

PHOTO BY TAM C. NGUYEN.

PHOTO BY TAM C. NGUYEN.

and these microfilariae circulate in the bloodstream, waiting to hitch a ride when the next mosquito bites. Once in the mosquito, the microfilariae develop into infective larvae and the entire process is repeated.

When dogs get infected with heartworm, over time they tend to develop symptoms associated with heart disease, such as coughing, exercise intolerance and potentially many other manifestations. Diagnosis is confirmed by either seeing the microfilariae themselves in blood samples or using immunologic tests (antigen testing) to identify the presence of adult heartworms. Since antigen tests measure the presence of adult heartworms and microfilarial tests measure offspring produced by adults, neither are positive until six to seven months after the initial infection. However, the beginning of damage can occur by fifth-stage larvae as early as three months after infection. Thus it is possible for dogs to be harboring problem-causing larvae for up to three months before either type of test would identify an infection.

The good news is that there are great protocols available for preventing heartworm in dogs. Testing is critical in the process, and it is important to understand the benefits as well as the limitations of such testing. All dogs six months of age or older that have not been on continuous heartworm-preventive medication

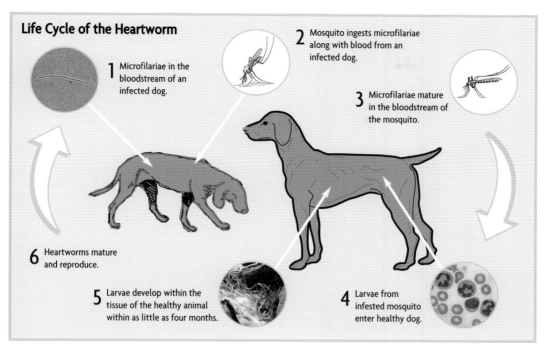

Life Cycle of the Heartworm

1 Microfilariae in the bloodstream of an infected dog.

2 Mosquito ingests microfilariae along with blood from an infected dog.

3 Microfilariae mature in the bloodstream of the mosquito.

6 Heartworms mature and reproduce.

5 Larvae develop within the tissue of the healthy animal within as little as four months.

4 Larvae from infested mosquito enter healthy dog.

should be screened with microfilarial or antigen tests. For dogs receiving preventive medication, periodic antigen testing helps assess the effectiveness of the preventives. Your veterinarian will likely have specific guidelines under which heartworm preventives will be prescribed, and many prefer to err on the side of safety and retest annually even if continous heartworm prevention has been provided.

It is indeed fortunate that heartworm is relatively easy to prevent, because treatments can be as life-threatening as the disease itself. Treatment requires a two-step process that kills the adult heartworms first and then the microfilariae. Prevention is obviously preferable; this involves a once-monthly oral or topical treatment. The popular wormer ivermectin (also sometimes used to treat *Demodex* infestation), has had deadly side effects in Collies and other herding breeds, so explore other options for your Beardie. Other choices include moxidectin and milbemycin oxime; the once-a-month topical drug selamectin provides heartworm protection in addition to flea, some types of tick and other parasite controls. Some Beardies do better on a daily preventive; discuss all of this with your vet.

THE **ABC**S OF
Emergency Care

Abrasions

Clean wound with running water or 3% hydrogen peroxide. Pat dry with gauze and spray with antibiotic. Do not cover.

Animal Bites

Clean area with soap and saline solution or water. Apply pressure to any bleeding area. Apply antibiotic ointment. Identify animal and contact vet.

Antifreeze Poisoning

Induce vomiting and take dog to the vet.

Bee Sting

Remove stinger and apply soothing lotion or cold compress; give antihistamine in proper dosage.

Bleeding

Apply pressure directly to wound with gauze or towel for five to ten minutes. If wound does not stop bleeding, wrap wound with gauze and adhesive tape.

Bloat/Gastric Torsion

Immediately take the dog to the vet or emergency clinic; phone from car. No time to waste.

Burns

Chemical: Bathe dog with water and pet shampoo. Rinse in saline solution. Apply antibiotic ointment.

Acid: Rinse with water. Apply one part baking soda, two parts water to affected area.

Alkali: Rinse with water. Apply one part vinegar, four parts water to affected area.

Electrical: Apply antibiotic ointment. Seek veterinary assistance immediately.

Choking

If the dog is on the verge of collapsing, wedge a solid object, such as the handle of screwdriver, between molars on one side of mouth to keep mouth open. Pull tongue out. Use long-nosed pliers or fingers to remove foreign object. Do not push the object down the dog's throat. For small or medium dogs, hold dog upside down by hind legs and shake firmly to dislodge foreign object.

Chlorine Ingestion

With clean water, rinse the mouth and eyes. Give dog water to drink; contact the vet.

Constipation

Feed dog 2 tablespoons bran flakes with each meal. Encourage drinking water. Mix $1/4$ teaspoon mineral oil in dog's food.

Diarrhea

Withhold food for 12 to 24 hours. Feed dog anti-diarrheal with eyedropper. When feeding resumes, feed one part boiled hamburger, one part plain cooked rice, $1/4$ to $3/4$ cup four times daily.

Dog Bite

Snip away hair around puncture wound; clean with 3% hydrogen peroxide; apply tincture of iodine. If wound appears deep, take the dog to the vet.

Frostbite

Wrap the dog in a heavy blanket. Warm affected area with a warm bath for ten minutes. Red color to skin will return with circulation; if tissues are pale after 20 minutes, contact the vet.

Use a portable, durable container large enough to contain all items.

DOG OWNER'S FIRST-AID KIT

- ❏ **Gauze bandages/swabs**
- ❏ **Adhesive and non-adhesive bandages**
- ❏ **Antibiotic powder**
- ❏ **Antiseptic wash**
- ❏ **Hydrogen peroxide 3%**
- ❏ **Antibiotic ointment**
- ❏ **Lubricating jelly**
- ❏ **Rectal thermometer**
- ❏ **Nylon muzzle**
- ❏ **Scissors and forceps**
- ❏ **Eyedropper**
- ❏ **Syringe**
- ❏ **Anti-bacterial/fungal solution**
- ❏ **Saline solution**
- ❏ **Antihistamine**
- ❏ **Cotton balls**
- ❏ **Nail clippers**
- ❏ **Screwdriver/pen knife**
- ❏ **Flashlight**
- ❏ **Emergency phone numbers**

Heat Stroke
Submerge the dog (up to his muzzle) in cold water; if no response within ten minutes, contact the vet.

Hot Spots
Mix 2 packets Domeboro® with 2 cups water. Saturate cloth with mixture and apply to hot spots for 15–30 minutes. Apply antibiotic ointment. Repeat every six to eight hours.

Poisonous Plants
Wash affected area with soap and water. Cleanse with alcohol. For foxtail/grass, apply antibiotic ointment. If ingested, contact the vet.

Rat Poison Ingestion
Induce vomiting. Keep dog calm, maintain dog's normal body temperature (use blanket or heating pad). Get to the vet for antidote.

Shock
Keep the dog calm and warm; call for veterinary assistance.

Snake Bite
If possible, bandage the area and apply pressure. If the area is not conducive to bandaging, use ice to control bleeding. Get immediate help from the vet.

Tick Removal
Apply flea and tick spray directly on tick. Wait one minute. Using tweezers or wearing plastic gloves, grasp the tick's body firmly. Apply antibiotic ointment.

Vomiting
Restrict dog's water intake; offer a few ice cubes. Withhold food for next meal. Contact vet if vomiting persists longer than 24 hours.

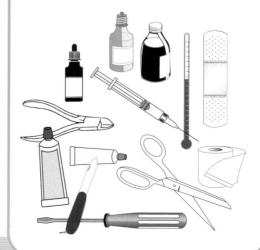

Number-One Killer Disease in Dogs: CANCER

In every age, there is a word associated with a disease or plague that causes humans to shudder. In the 21st century, that word is "cancer." Just as cancer is the leading cause of death in humans, it claims nearly half the lives of all dogs that die from a natural disease as well as half the dogs that die over the age of ten years.

Described as a genetic disease, cancer becomes a greater risk as the dog ages. Vets and dog owners have become increasingly aware of the threat of cancer to dogs. Statistics reveal that one dog in every five will develop cancer, the most common of which is skin cancer. Many cancers, including prostate, ovarian and breast cancer, can be avoided by spaying and neutering our dogs by the age of six months.

Early detection of cancer can save or extend a dog's life, so it is absolutely vital for owners to have their dogs examined by a qualified vet or oncologist immediately upon detection of any abnormality. Certain dietary guidelines have also proven to reduce the onset and spread of cancer. Foods based on fish rather than beef, due to the presence of Omega-3 fatty acids, are recommended. Other amino acids such as glutamine have significant benefits for canines, particularly those breeds that show a greater susceptibility to cancer.

Cancer management and treatments promise hope for future generations of canines. Since the disease is genetic, breeders should never breed a dog whose parents, grandparents and any related siblings have developed cancer. It is difficult to know whether to exclude an otherwise healthy dog from a breeding program, as the disease does not manifest itself until the dog's senior years.

RECOGNIZE CANCER WARNING SIGNS

Since early detection can possibly rescue your dog from becoming a cancer statistic, it is essential for owners to recognize the possible signs and seek the assistance of a qualified professional.

- Abnormal bumps or lumps that continue to grow
- Bleeding or discharge from any body cavity
- Persistent stiffness or lameness
- Recurrent sores or sores that do not heal
- Inappetence
- Breathing difficulties
- Weight loss
- Bad breath or odors
- General malaise and fatigue
- Eating and swallowing problems
- Difficulty urinating and defecating

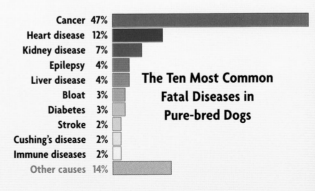

Cancer	47%
Heart disease	12%
Kidney disease	7%
Epilepsy	4%
Liver disease	4%
Bloat	3%
Diabetes	3%
Stroke	2%
Cushing's disease	2%
Immune diseases	2%
Other causes	14%

The Ten Most Common Fatal Diseases in Pure-bred Dogs

CDS: Cognitive Dysfunction Syndrome

"Old-Dog Syndrome"

There are many ways for you to evaluate old-dog syndrome. Veterinarians have defined CDS (cognitive dysfunction syndrome) as the gradual deterioration of cognitive abilities, indicated by changes in the dog's behavior. When a dog changes his routine response, and maladies have been eliminated as the cause of these behavioral changes, then CDS is the usual diagnosis.

More than half the dogs over eight years old suffer from some form of CDS. The older the dog, the more chance he has of suffering from CDS. In humans, doctors often dismiss the CDS behavioral changes as part of "winding down."

There are four major signs of CDS: frequent potty accidents inside the home, sleeping much more or much less than normal, acting confused and failing to respond to social stimuli.

Symptoms of CDS

FREQUENT POTTY ACCIDENTS
- Urinates in the house.
- Defecates in the house.
- Doesn't signal that he wants to go out.

FAILURE TO RESPOND TO SOCIAL STIMULI
- Comes to people less frequently, whether called or not.
- Doesn't tolerate petting for more than a short time.
- Doesn't come to the door when you return home.

CONFUSION
- Goes outside and just stands there.
- Appears confused with a faraway look in his eyes.
- Hides more often.
- Doesn't recognize friends.
- Doesn't come when called.
- Walks around listlessly and without a destination.

SLEEP PATTERNS
- Awakens more slowly.
- Sleeps more than normal during the day.
- Sleeps less during the night.

BEARDED COLLIE

AKC CONFORMATION SHOWING

Is dog showing in your blood? Are you excited by the idea of gaiting your handsome Bearded Collie around the ring to the thunderous applause of an enthusiastic audience? Are you certain that your beloved Bearded Collie is flawless? You are not alone!

Success in the show ring, however, requires more than a pretty face, a waggy tail and a pocketful of liver. Even though dog shows can be exciting and enjoyable, the sport of conformation makes great demands on the exhibitors and the dogs. Winning exhibitors live for their dogs, devoting time and money to their dogs' presentation, conditioning and training. Very few novices, even those with good dogs, will find themselves in the winners' circle, though it does happen. Don't be disheartened, though. Every exhibitor began as a novice and worked his way up to the Group ring (for Beardies, the Herding Group). It's the "working your way up" part that you must keep in mind.

Many owners start by entering their Beardies in dog shows for the fun and enjoyment of it. Dog showing makes an absorbing hobby, with many rewards for dogs and owners alike. If you're having fun, meeting other people who share your interests and enjoying the overall experience, you likely will catch the "bug." Once the dog-show bug bites, its effects can last a lifetime; it's certainly much better than a deer tick! Soon you will be envisioning yourself in the center ring at the Westminster Kennel Club Dog Show in New York City, competing for the prestigious Best in Show cup. This magical dog show is televised annually from Madison Square Garden, and the victorious dog becomes a celebrity overnight.

Visiting a dog show as a spectator is a great place to start. Pick up the show catalog to find out what time your breed is being shown, who is judging the breed and in which ring the classes will be held. To start, Bearded Collies compete against other Bearded Collies, and the winner is selected as Best of Breed by the judge. This is the procedure for each breed. At a group show, all of the Best of Breed winners go on to compete for Group One in their respective groups. For example, all Best of Breed winners in a given group compete against each other; this is done for all seven groups. Finally, all seven group winners go head to head in the ring for the Best in Show award.

What most spectators don't understand is the basic idea of conformation. A dog show is often referred to as a "conformation" show. This means that the judge should decide how each dog stacks up (conforms) to the breed standard for his given breed: how well does this Bearded Collie conform to the ideal representative detailed in the standard? Ideally, this is what happens. In reality, however, this ideal often gets slighted as the judge compares Bearded Collie #1 to Bearded Collie #2. Again, the ideal is that each dog is judged based on his merits in comparison to his breed standard, not in comparison to the other dogs in the ring.

It is easier for judges to compare dogs of the same breed to decide which they think is the better specimen; in the Group and Best in Show ring, however, it is very difficult to compare one breed to another, like apples to oranges. Thus the dog's conformation to the breed standard—not to mention advertising dollars and good handling—is essential to success in conformation shows. The dog described in the standard (the standard for each AKC breed is written and approved by the breed's national parent club and

If you are interested in showing your Bearded Collie, it would be a good idea to go to one or two shows in order to get a feel for what goes on and how show dogs look and act.

then submitted to the AKC for approval) is the perfect dog of that breed, and breeders keep their eye on the standard when they choose which dogs to breed, hoping to get

BECOMING A CHAMPION

An official AKC championship of record requires that a dog accumulate 15 points under three different judges, including two "majors" under different judges. Points are awarded based on the number of dogs entered into competition, varying from breed to breed and place to place. A win of three, four or five points is considered a "major." The AKC annually assigns a schedule of points to adjust to variations that accompany a breed's popularity and the population of a given area.

closer and closer to the ideal with each litter.

Another good first step for the novice is to join a dog club. You will be astonished by the many and different kinds of dog clubs in the country, with about 5,000 clubs holding events every year. A parent club is the national organization, sanctioned by the AKC, which promotes and safeguards its breed in the country. The Bearded Collie Club of America can be contacted on the Internet at http://beardie.net/bcca. The parent club holds an annual national specialty show, usually in a different city each year, in which many of the country's top dogs, handlers and breeders gather to compete. At a specialty show, only members of a single breed are invited to participate. There are also group specialties, in which all members of a group are invited. For more information about dog clubs in your area, search the AKC's website at www.akc.org or write them at their Raleigh, NC address.

OBEDIENCE TRIALS

Mrs. Helen Whitehouse Walker, a Standard Poodle fancier, can be credited with introducing obedience trials to the United States. In the 1930s, she designed a series of exercises based on those of the Associated Sheep, Police, Army Dog Society of Great Britain. These exercises were intended to evaluate the working relationship between dog and owner. Since those early days of the sport in the US, obedience trials have grown more and more popular, and now more than 2,000 trials each year attract over 100,000 dogs and their owners. Any dog registered with the AKC, regardless of neutering or other disqualifications that would preclude entry in conformation competition, can participate in obedience trials.

A dog must complete different exercises at each level of obedience. The Novice exercises are the

FIVE CLASSES AT SHOWS

At most AKC all-breed shows, there are five regular classes offered: Puppy, Novice, Bred-by-Exhibitor, American-bred and Open. The Puppy Class is usually divided as 6 to 9 months of age and 9 to 12 months of age. When deciding in which class to enter your dog, whether male or female, you must carefully check the show schedule to make sure that you have selected the right class. Depending on the age of the dog, its previous first-place wins and the sex of the dog, you must make the best choice. It is possible to enter a one-year-old dog who has not won sufficient first places in any of the non-Puppy Classes, though the competition is more intense the further you progress from the Puppy Class.

easiest, with the Open and finally the Utility levels progressing in difficulty. Examples of Novice exercises are on- and off-lead heeling, a figure-8 pattern, performing a recall (or come), long sit, long down and standing for examination. In the Open level, the Novice-level exercises are required again, but this time without a leash and for longer durations. In addition, the dog must clear a broad jump, retrieve over a jump and drop on recall. In the Utility level, the exercises are quite difficult, including executing basic commands based on hand signals, following a complex heeling pattern, locating articles based on scent discrimination and completing jumps at the handler's direction.

A historical win for the breed at England's Crufts Dog Show. This Bearded Collie won Best of Breed and was the first dog ever to win the newly designated Pastoral Group (akin to the AKC's Herding Group) in 1999.

OTHER TYPES OF COMPETITION

In addition to conformation shows, the AKC holds a variety of other competitive events. Obedience trials, agility trials and tracking trials are open to all breeds, while hunting tests, field trials, lure coursing, herding tests and trials, earthdog tests and coonhound events are limited to specific breeds or groups of breeds. The Junior Showmanship program is offered to aspiring young handlers and their dogs, and the Canine Good Citizen® program is an all-around good-behavior test open to all dogs, pure-bred and mixed.

AGILITY TRIALS

Agility trials became sanctioned by the AKC in August 1994, when the first licensed agility trials were held. Since that time, agility certainly has grown in popularity by leaps and bounds, literally! The AKC allows all registered breeds (including Miscellaneous Class breeds) to participate, providing the dog is 12 months of age or older. Agility is designed so that the handler demonstrates how well the dog can work at his side. The handler directs his dog through, over, under and around an obstacle course that includes jumps, tires, the dog walk, weave poles, pipe tunnels, collapsed tunnels and more. While working his way through the course, the dog must keep one eye and ear on the handler and the rest of his body on the course. The handler runs along with the dog, giving verbal and hand signals to guide the dog through the course.

The first organization to promote agility trials in the US was the United States Dog Agility Association, Inc. (USDAA). Established in 1986, the USDAA sparked the formation of many member clubs around the country. To participate in USDAA trials, dogs must be at least 18 months of age. The USDAA and AKC both offer titles to winning dogs, although the exercises and requirements of the two organizations differ.

Agility trials are a great way to keep your dog active, and they will keep you running, too! You should join a local agility club to learn more about the sport. These clubs offer sessions in which you can introduce your dog to the various obstacles as well as training classes to prepare him for competition. In no time, your dog will be climbing A-frames, crossing the dog walk and flying over hurdles, all with you right beside him. Your heart will leap every time your dog jumps through the hoop—and you'll be having just as much (if not more) fun!

TRACKING

Tracking tests are exciting ways to test your Bearded Collie's instinctive scenting ability on a competitive level. All dogs have a nose, and all breeds are welcome in tracking tests. The first AKC-licensed tracking test took place in 1937 as part of the Utility level at an obedience trial, and thus competitive tracking was officially begun. The first title, Tracking Dog (TD), was offered in 1947, ten years after the first official tracking test. It was not until 1980 that the AKC added the title Tracking Dog Excellent (TDX), which was followed by the title Versatile Surface Tracking (VST) in 1995. Champion Tracker (CT) is awarded to a dog who has earned all three of those titles.

HERDING EVENTS

The first recorded sheepdog trial was held in Wales in the late 19th century; since then, the popularity of herding events has grown around the world. The AKC began offering herding events in 1989, and participation is open to all breeds in the Herding Group as well as Rottweilers and Samoyeds. These events are designed to evaluate the dogs' herding instincts, and the aim is to develop these innate skills and show that herding dogs today can still perform the functions for which they were originally

intended, whether or not they are actually used in working capacities. Herding events are designed to simulate farm situations and are held on two levels: tests and trials.

AKC herding tests are more basic and are scored on a pass/fail system, meaning that dogs do not compete against each other to earn titles. Titles at this level are Herding Tested (HT) and the more difficult Pre-Trial Tested (PT). In addition, there is a non-competitive certification program, Herding Instinct Tested, which gives you a chance to evaluate the potential that your dog may have for herding. If your dog successfully passes this test, he receives a Herding Instinct Certificate, which makes him eligible to enter herding trials.

The more challenging herding trial level is competitive and requires more training and experience. There are three different courses (A, B and C, each with a different type of farm situation) with different types of livestock (cattle, sheep or ducks). There are three titles available on each course, Herding Started, Herding Intermediate and Herding Advanced, with each level being progressively more difficult. The type of course and type of livestock used for the trial are based on the given breed's typical use. Once a Herding Advanced title has been earned on a course, the dog can then begin to strive for the Herding Champion title.

In addition to events held by the AKC, breed clubs often hold herding events for these breeds. Other specialty organizations hold trials that are open to all herding breeds; the way these events are structured and the titles that are awarded differ from those of the AKC. For example, the American Herding Breed Association (AHBA) allows any breed with herding in its ancestry to participate, as well as allowing mixed-breed herding dogs. To pass the Herding Instinct Test, the handler works with the dog at the shepherd's direction while the shepherd evaluates the dog's willingness to approach, move and round up the sheep while at the same time following the instructions of his handler.

At the competition level in AHBA events, dogs work with their handlers to move sheep up and down the field, through gates and into a pen, and also to hold the sheep without a pen, all while being timed. This is an amazing sight to see! A good dog working with the shepherd has to be the ultimate man-dog interaction. Rare breeds were often traditionally used for herding and, fortunately, the AHBA is more than happy to have rare breeds participate. Club members and spectators love to welcome some of these wonderful dogs that they have only read about but never seen.

BEARDED COLLIE

You chose your dog because something clicked the minute you set eyes on him. Or perhaps it seemed that the dog selected you and that's what clinched the deal. Either way, you are now investing time and money in this dog, a true pal and an outstanding member of the family. Everything about him is perfect...well, almost perfect. Remember, he is a dog! For that matter, how does he think *you're* doing?

UNDERSTANDING THE CANINE MINDSET

For starters, you and your dog are on different wavelengths. Your dog is similar to a toddler in that both live in the present tense only. A dog's view of life is based primarily on cause and effect, which is similar to the old saying,

"Nothing teaches a youngster to hang on like falling off the swing." If your dog stumbles down a flight of three steps, the next time he will either approach the stairs more carefully or avoid the steps altogether.

Your dog makes connections based on the fact that he lives in the present, so when he is doing something and you interrupt to dispense praise or a correction, a connection, positive or negative, is made. To the dog, that's like one plus one equals two! In the same sense, it's also easy to see that when your timing is off, you will cause an incorrect connection. The one-plus-one way of thinking is why you must never scold a dog for behavior that took place an hour, 15 minutes or even 5 seconds ago. But it is also why, when your timing is perfect, you can teach him to do all kinds of wonderful things—as soon as he has made that essential connection. What helps the process is his desire to please you and to have your approval.

There are behaviors we admire in dogs, such as friendliness and obedience, as well as those behaviors that cause problems to a varying degree. The dog

Communicating with your dog properly and understanding his communications with you are keys to a loving, mutually rewarding friendship.

owner who encounters minor behavioral problems is wise to solve them promptly or get professional help. Bad behaviors are not corrected by repeatedly shouting "No" or getting angry with the dog. Only the giving of praise and approval for good behavior lets your dog understand right from wrong. The longer a bad behavior is allowed to continue, the harder it is to overcome. A responsible breeder is often able to help. Each dog is unique, so try not to compare your dog's behavior with your neighbor's dog or the one you had as a child.

Have your veterinarian check the dog to see whether a behavior problem could have a physical cause. An earache or toothache, for example, could be the reason for a dog to snap at you if you were to touch his head when putting on his leash. A sharp correction from you would only

increase the behavior. When a physical basis is eliminated, and if the problem is not something you understand or can cope with, ask for the name of a behavioral specialist, preferably one who is familiar with the Bearded Collie. Be sure to keep the breeder informed of your progress.

Many things, such as environment and inherited traits, form the basic behavior of a dog, just as in humans. You also must factor into his temperament the purpose for which your dog was originally

Beardies can be the most exuberant greeters in the dog world. Owners usually enjoy their Beardies' eager hellos, but it is best to curtail this behavior from puppyhood, as not everyone your dog meets will appreciate it.

PROFESSIONAL HELP

Every trainer and behaviorist asks, "Why didn't you come to me sooner?" Pet owners often don't want to admit that anything is wrong with their dogs. A dog's problem often is due to the dog and his owner mixing their messages, which will only get worse. Don't put it off; consult a professional to find out whether or not the problem is serious enough to require intervention.

greeting may be, the chances are that your visitors will not appreciate your dog's bouncing, boundless enthusiasm. The dog will not be able to distinguish upon whom he can jump and whom he cannot. Therefore, it is probably best to discourage this behavior entirely.

Pick a command such as "Off" (avoid using "Down" since you will use that for the dog to lie down) and tell him "Off" when he jumps up. Place him on the ground on all fours and have him sit, praising him the whole time. Always lavish him with praise and petting when he is in the sit position. That way, you are still giving him a warm affectionate greeting because you are as excited to see him as he is to see you!

BARKING
Giving voice, a.k.a. barking, is a bred-for characteristic of the working Bearded Collie. As the Beardie herds his fleecy charges, he instinctively gives voice, communicating with both the sheep and his master (the shepherd). There is no doubt that every Beardie has a lot to say—regardless of whether he's been asked. Whatever it is that the dog is trying to say, he should not be punished for barking.

In our modern societies, where Beardies rarely herd anything other than the family cat and bedroom slippers, a barky

Chewing can be a problem, especially if your dog starts to ruin your belongings. Provide proper chew toys for your Bearded Collie to encourage constructive chewing habits.

bred. The major obstacle lies in the dog's inability to explain his behavior to us in a way that we understand. The one thing you should not do is to give up and abandon your dog. Somewhere a misunderstanding has occurred but, with help and patient understanding on your part, you should be able to work out the majority of bothersome behaviors.

JUMPING UP
For the Beardie, jumping up is more than friendly way of saying hello—it is an essential way of life! Some dog owners do not mind when their Beardies jump up, loving this eager greeting. Nonetheless, a problem arises when guests come to the house and the dog greets them in the same manner—whether they like it or not. However friendly the

Beardie is not desirable. It will be necessary to redirect the Beardie pup's barking from the very beginning, or else your Beardie might be hosting his own talk show in no time at all...and your neighbors will not tune in with much amusement.

Fortunately, Beardies tend to use their barks more purposefully than most other dogs and thereby can be taught when to bark and when not to bark. For example, if an intruder came into your home in the middle of the night and your Bearded Collie barked a warning, wouldn't you be pleased? You would probably deem your dog a hero, a wonderful guardian and protector of the home. Most dogs are not as discriminating as the Bearded Collie.

On the other hand, if a friend drops by unexpectedly, rings the

GIMME WHEELS!

Chasing cars or bikes is dangerous for all parties concerned: dogs, drivers and cyclists. Something about those wheels going around fascinates dogs, but that fascination can end in disastrous results. Corrections for your dog's chasing behavior must be immediate and firm. Tell him "Leave it!" and then give him either a sit or a down command. Get kids on bikes to help saturate your dog with spinning wheels while he politely practices his sits and downs.

doorbell and is greeted with a sudden sharp bark, you would probably be annoyed at the dog. But in reality, isn't this just the same behavior? The dog does not know any better...unless he sees who is at the door and it is someone he knows, he will bark as a means of vocalizing that his (and your) territory is being threatened. While your friend is not posing a threat, it is all the same to the dog. Barking is his means of letting you know that there is an intrusion, whether friend or foe, on your property. This type of barking is instinctive and should not be discouraged. Let your Beardie know when his bark is appropriate and when it is not.

Excessive habitual barking, however, is a problem that should be corrected early on. As your Bearded Collie grows up, you will be able to tell when his barking is purposeful and when it is for no reason. You will become able to distinguish your dog's different barks and their meanings. For example, the bark when someone comes to the door will be different from the bark when he is excited to see you. It is similar to a person's tone of voice, except that the dog has to rely totally on tone of voice because he does not have the benefit of using words. An incessant barker will be evident at an early age.

There are some things that encourage a dog to bark. For

By making your Beardie wait for his food and by creating boundaries for him with proper use of his crate, you are reinforcing your pack-leader status.

aggression, but all are degrees of dominance, indicating that the dog, not his master, is (or thinks he is) in control. When the dog feels that he (or his control of the situation) is threatened, he will respond. The extent of the aggressive behavior varies with individual dogs. It is not at all pleasant to see bared teeth or to hear your dog growl or snarl, but these are signs of behavior that, if left uncorrected, can become extremely dangerous. A word of warning here: never challenge an aggressive dog. He is unpredictable and therefore unreliable to approach. Fortunately for Beardie owners, their breed is a naturally friendly one, but all responsible dog owners should know about aggression.

Nothing gets a "hello" from strangers on the street quicker than walking a puppy, but people should ask permission before petting your dog so you can tell him to sit in order to receive the admiring pats. If a hand comes down over the dog's head and he shrinks back, ask the person to bring their hand up, underneath the pup's chin. Now you're correcting strangers, too! But if you don't, it could make your dog afraid of strangers, which in turn can lead to fear-biting. Socialization prevents much aggression before it rears its ugly head.

The body language of an aggressive dog about to attack is

example, if your dog barks non-stop for a few minutes and you give him a treat to quiet him, he believes that you are rewarding him for barking and he will keep doing it. However, if you issue a "Quiet" command and give the treat when he stops barking, he will learn what "Quiet" means.

AGGRESSION

"Aggression" is a word that is often misunderstood and is sometimes even used to describe what is actually normal canine behavior. For example, it's normal for puppies to growl when playing tug-of-war. It's puppy talk. There are different forms of dog clear. The dog will have a hard, steady stare. He will try to look as big as possible by standing stiff-legged, pushing out his chest, keeping his ears up and holding his tail up and steady. The hackles on his back will rise so that a ridge of hairs stands up. This posture may include the curled lip, snarl and/or growl, or he may be silent. He looks, and definitely is, very dangerous.

This dominant posture is seen in dogs that are territorially aggressive. Deliverymen are constant victims of serious bites from such dogs. Territorial aggression is the reason you should never, ever, try to train a puppy to be a watchdog. It can escalate into this type of behavior over which you will have no control. All forms of aggression must be taken seriously and dealt with immediately. If signs of aggressive behav-

Beardies generally enjoy the company of cats, especially if socialized with them from puppyhood. However, the family cat might not know what to make of the Beardie's boisterous nature.

ior continue or grow worse, or if you are at all unsure about how to deal with your dog's behavior, get the help of a professional.

Uncontrolled aggression, sometimes called "irritable aggression," is not something for the pet owner to try to solve. If you cannot solve your dog's dangerous behavior with professional help, and you (quite rightly) do not wish to keep a canine time-bomb in your home, you will have some important decisions to make. Aggressive dogs often cannot be rehomed successfully, as they are dangerous and unreliable in their behavior. An aggressive dog should be dealt with only by someone who knows exactly the situation that he is getting into and has the

DOMINANCE

Dogs are born with dominance skills, meaning that they can be quite clever in trying to get their way. The "follow-me" trot to the cookie jar is an example. The toy dropped in your lap says "Play with me." The leash delivered to you along with an excited look means "Take me for a walk." These are all good-natured dominant behaviors. Ask your dog to sit before agreeing to his request and you'll remain "top dog."

When beginning commands with your pup, always have him on lead to keep him close and paying attention.

experience, dedication and ideal living environment to attempt rehabilitating the dog, which often is not possible. In these cases, the dog ends up having to be humanely put down. Making a decision about euthanasia is not an easy undertaking for anyone, for any reason; hopefully, as a Beardie owner, this is a situation you will never have to face.

GET A WHIFF OF HIM!

Dogs sniff each others' rears as their way of saying "hi" as well as to find out who the other dog is and how he's doing. That's normal behavior between canines, but it can, annoyingly, extend to people. The command for all unwanted sniffing is "Leave it!" Give the command in a no-nonsense voice and move on.

A milder form of aggression is the dog's guarding anything that he perceives to be his—his food dish, his toys, his bed and/or his crate. This can be prevented if you take firm control from the start. The young puppy can and should be taught that his leader will share, but that certain rules apply. Guarding is mild aggression only in the beginning stages, and it will worsen and become dangerous if you let it.

Don't try to snatch anything away from your puppy. Bargain for the item in question by offering a treat or another toy so that you can positively reinforce him when he gives it up. Punishment only results in worsening any aggressive behavior.

Many dogs extend their guarding impulse toward items they've stolen. The dog figures, "If I have it, it's mine!" (Some ill-behaved kids have similar tendencies.) An angry confrontation will only increase the dog's aggression. (Have you ever watched a child have a tantrum?) Try a simple distraction first, such as tossing a toy or picking up his leash for a walk. If that doesn't work, the best way to handle the situation is with basic obedience. Show the dog a treat, followed by calm, almost slow-motion commands: "Come. Sit. Drop it. Good dog," and then hand over the cheese! That's one example of positive-reinforcement training.

Children can be bitten when they try to retrieve a stolen shoe or toy, so they need to know how to handle the dog or to let an adult do it. They may also be bitten as they run away from a dog, in either fear or play. The dog sees the child's running as reason for pursuit, and even a friendly young puppy will nip at

the heels of a runaway. Teach the kids not to run away from a strange dog and when to stop overly exciting play with their own puppy.

Fear biting is yet another aggressive behavior. A fear biter gives many warning signals. The dog leans away from the approaching person (sometimes hiding behind his owner) with his ears and tail down, but not in submission. He may even shiver. His hackles are raised, his lips curled. When the person steps into the dog's "flight zone" (a circle of 1 to 3 feet surrounding the dog), he attacks. Because of the fear factor, he performs a rapid attack-and-retreat. Because it is directed at a person, vets are often the victims of this form of aggression. It is frightening, but discovering and eliminating the cause of

Food stealing doesn't happen only in the kitchen! A Beardie will follow his nose wherever a tantalizing scent takes him.

JEALOUS PETS

In households with more than one pet, one pet must be dominant. This means that one pet gets more attention, sits closest to you, goes out the door first, takes up more room on the bed and in hundreds of other tiny ways exerts his dominance. The pets will occasionally squabble over your unintended partiality, but it's best not to interfere.

the fright will help overcome the dog's need to bite. Early socialization again plays a strong role in the prevention of this behavior. Again, if you can't cope with it, get the help of an expert.

SEPARATION ANXIETY
Any behaviorist will tell you that separation anxiety is the most common problem about which pet owners complain. It is also one of the easiest to prevent. Unfortunately, a behaviorist usually is not consulted until the dog is a stressed-out, neurotic mess. At that stage, it is indeed a problem that requires the help of a professional.

Training the puppy to the fact that people in the house come and go is essential in order to avoid this anxiety. Leaving the puppy in his crate or a confined area while family members go in and out, and stay out for longer and longer periods of time, is the basic way to desensitize the pup to the family's frequent departures. If you are at home most of every day, make it a point to go out for at least an hour or two whenever possible.

How you leave is vital to the dog's reaction. Your dog is no fool. He knows the difference between sweats and business suits, jeans and dresses. He sees you pat your pocket to check for your wallet, open your briefcase, check that you have your cell phone or pick

THE MACHO DOG
The Venus/Mars differences are found in dogs, too. Males have distinct behaviors that, while seemingly sex-related, are more closely connected to the role of the male as leader. Marking territory by urinating on it is one means that male dogs use to establish their presence. Doing so merely says, "I've been here." Small dogs often attempt to lift their legs higher on the tree than the previous male. While this is natural behavior outdoors on items like telephone poles, fence posts, fire hydrants and most other upright objects, marking indoors is totally unacceptable. Treat it as you would a house-training accident and clean thoroughly to eradicate the scent.

Another behavior often seen in the macho male, mounting is a dominance display. Neutering the dog before six months of age helps to deter this behavior. You can discourage him from mounting by catching the dog as he's about to mount you, stepping quickly aside and saying "Off!"

up the car keys. He knows from the hurry of the kids in the morning that they're off to school until afternoon. Lipstick? Aftershave lotion? Lunch boxes? Every move you make registers in his sensory perception and memory. Your puppy knows more about your departures than anyone else. You can't get away with a thing!

Before you got dressed, you checked the dog's water bowl and his supply of safe chew toys, and you turned the radio on low. You will leave him in what he considers his "safe" area, not with total freedom of the house. If you've invested in child safety gates, you can be reasonably sure that he'll remain in the designated area. Don't give him access to a window where he can watch you leave the house. If you're leaving for an hour or two, just put him into his crate with a safe toy.

Now comes the test! You are ready to walk out the door. Do not give your Bearded Collie a big hug and a fond farewell. Do not drag out a long goodbye. Those are the very things that jump-start separation anxiety. Toss a biscuit into the dog's area, call out "So long, pooch" and close the door. You're gone. The chances are that the dog may bark a couple of times, or maybe whine once or twice, and then settle down to enjoy his biscuit and take a lovely nap, especially if you took him for a nice long walk before you left. As he grows up, the barks and whines will stop because it's an old routine, so why should he make the effort?

When you first brought home the puppy, the come-and-go routine was intermittent and constant. He was put into his crate with a tiny treat. You left (silently) and returned in 3

Your Bearded Collie loves your company. If dogs are left alone too much, they can suffer from separation anxiety.

minutes, then 5, then 10, then 15, then half an hour, until finally you could leave without a problem and be gone for 2 or 3 hours. If, at any time in the future, there's a "separation" problem, refresh his memory by going back to that basic training.

Now comes the next most important part—your return. Do not make a big production of coming home. "Hi, poochie" is as grand a greeting as he needs. When you've taken off your hat and coat, tossed your briefcase on the hall table and glanced at the mail, and the dog has settled down from the excitement of seeing you "in person" from his confined area, then go and give him a warm, friendly greeting. A potty trip is needed and a walk

Bearded Collies depend on the love and affection they receive from their human families.

would be appreciated, since he's been such a good dog.

DIGGING

Digging is natural and normal doggy behavior. Wild canines dig to bury whatever food they can save for later to eat. (And you thought *we* invented the doggie bag!) Burying bones or toys is a primary cause to dig. Dogs also dig to get at interesting little underground creatures like moles and mice. In the summer, they dig to get down to cool earth. In winter, they dig to get beneath the cold surface to warmer earth.

The solution to the last two is easy. In the summer, provide a bed that's up off the ground and placed in a shaded area. In winter,

the dog should either be indoors to sleep or given an adequate insulated doghouse outdoors. To understand how natural and normal this is, you have only to

"LEAVE IT"

Watch your puppy like a hawk to be certain it's a toy he's chewing, not your wallet. When you catch him in the act, tell him "Leave it!" and substitute a proper toy. Chewing on anything other than his own safe toys is countered by spraying the desirable (to the dog) object with a foul-tasting product like Bitter Apple and being more diligent in your observations of his chewing habits. When you can't supervise, it's crate time for Fido.

consider the Nordic breeds of sled dog who, at the end of the run, routinely dig a bed for themselves in the snow. It's the nesting instinct. How often have you seen your dog go round and round in circles, pawing at his blanket or bedding before flopping down to sleep?

Domesticated dogs also dig to escape, and that's a lot more dangerous than it is destructive. A dog that digs under the fence is the one that is hit by a car or becomes lost. A good fence to protect a digger should be set 12 inches below ground level, and every fence needs to be

Watch your Beardie carefully to prevent him from picking up and ingesting foreign objects from the ground. Dogs find the strangest things tasty!

routinely checked for even the smallest openings that can become possible escape routes.

Catching your dog in the act of digging is the easiest way to stop it, because your dog will make the "one-plus-one" connection, but digging is too often a solitary occupation, something the lonely dog does out of boredom. Catch your young puppy in the act and put a stop to it before you have a yard full of craters. It is more difficult to stop if your dog sees you gardening. If you can dig, why can't he? Because you say so, that's why! Some dogs are excavation experts, and some dogs never dig. However, when it comes to any of these instinctive canine behaviors, never say "never."

STOP, THIEF!

The easiest way to prevent a dog from stealing food is to stop this behavior before it starts by never leaving food out where he can reach it. However, if it is too late and your dog has already made a steal, you must stop your furry felon from becoming a repeat offender. Once Sneaky Pete has successfully stolen food, place a bit of food where he can reach it. Place an empty soda can with some pebbles in it on top of the food. Leave the room and watch what happens. As the dog grabs the tasty morsel, the can comes with it. The noise of the tumbling pebble-filled can makes its own correction, and you don't have to say a word.

INDEX

Page numbers in **boldface** indicate illustrations.

:My Bearded Collie

PUT YOUR PUPPY'S FIRST PICTURE HERE

Dog's Name _____

Date _____ Photographer _____